CONTEN

CW00602376

INTRODUCTION

When I was approached about producing this book, it was the idea of themed tours that most appealed. To gather together a series of connected "attractions" that, in the course of a day, would enable the traveller to thoroughly enjoy his or her special interest.

Whether country crafts or Roman remains, maritime history or smoked fish, you will find it all in the following pages. There are ten main sections each divided into several tours. Each tour can be completed in a day, or shortened to suit the individual. If the weather is hot, to spend much of the day driving - albeit along Dorset's attractive byways - does not suit us all. Time has been allowed to explore the various venues and drive on but, if you find the perfect picnic spot, why not make a day of it?

Some of the places suggested as visits have an entrance fee and this is made clear in the text; many are free. There are one or two private houses which, mainly because of their appearance, are of interest; please respect the privacy of their owners.

Apart from the walks in Coast and Country where a larger scale map may be preferred, an overall leisure map of Dorset will be found to be most useful. Signposts can be few and far between. To find the enclosing banks getting steeper, the lanes becoming narrower with grass growing in the centre, does not encourage the belief that the sought-after major road is just around the corner! The individual maps showing the locations and spread of various places on each tour are, because of their small scale, approximate only.

There is a Geographical Index, so if you prefer to confine your explorations to one particular area it is easy to discover what else is in the vicinity. I have also included a list of Tourist Information Centres where you will find staff very willing to help with additional information.

I hope *"Escape into Dorset"* will take you somewhere you haven't been before and, if you are a visitor, that you will leave the county determined to come back. There is so much to see. Enjoy it - and may the sun shine every day.

LOST VILLAGES

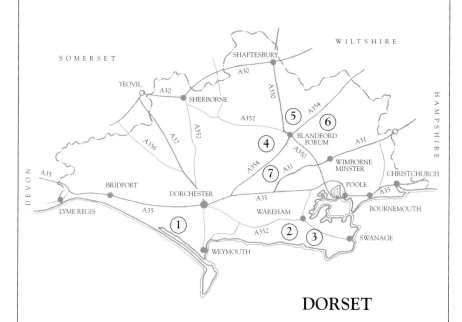

THE COASTAL TOUR
1. East Fleet
2. East Lulworth
3. Tyneham

THE INLAND TOUR
4. Milton Abbas
5. Gunvil Eastbury
6. Knowlton
7. Winterborne Tomson

LOST VILLAGES

There are more than two hundred lost villages of Dorset, whose fortunes can be gleaned from many sources. Books, maps, parish records and personal knowledge backed by extensive family histories all add pieces to a jigsaw of fascinating information. Some villages have gone forever; no trace remains. Others are represented by a ruin, a farmstead, or a manor house.

The reasons for their decline were various. Perhaps a falling water table on the chalk downs resulted in villagers moving nearer the source of water, leaving higher settlements abandoned. One or two villages were wiped out by plague while, on the coast, others suffered severe storm damage and were inundated by the sea. One famous Dorset village was demolished and rebuilt in a new location solely at the convenience of the local landowner.

While historians study grassy mounds and aerial photographs to pinpoint these old settlements, the holidaymaker prefers something more picturesque. Both these tours fit that criteria.

The Coastal Tour

EAST FLEET (1)

The pebble bank of Chesil Beach stretches along the coast from Portland to Abbotsbury and beyond, trapping behind it the "inland sea" known as the Fleet. At its eastern end, oyster beds provide delicacies for local restaurants; to the west, the Swannery enchants visitors both young and old, especially when the cygnets are hatching and taking their first swim on the placid Fleet.

Chesil Beach is an invaluable defence against stormy seas, but it has also proved a watery grave for mariners who, shipwrecked in the treacherous seas off Portland, were unable to scale the steep bank of sliding, smooth pebbles to gain the safety of the shore. It was on such a night of shipwreck that the village of East Fleet was swept away.

On 23 November 1824, according to an eye-witness report: "The sea began to break over the beach at 5 a.m. and the water came up as fast as a horse could gallop." The village, where evidence of settlement has been found from as long as 7,000 years ago, became the only village in the county to be destroyed by the sea. The tiny church tried to stand firm, but the nave could not withstand the battering. Only the chancel now remains.

Fleet was a known haunt of smugglers. It has seen a chequered ownership, but in 1566 passed to the Mohun family who held it for two centuries. The names Mohun and Fleet were linked by J. Meade Falkner in the 1880s and the resulting tale of smuggling and derring do in the village of "Moonfleet" is as exciting a read now as it was then.

The old church contains some interesting memorials. A track leads to the Coast

The ruined church at Fleet.

Path along the edge of the Fleet where, heading west, the Elm Tree pub at Langton Herring provides an excellent incentive to stretch your legs.

EAST LULWORTH (2)

The village of East Lulworth, south of the Dorchester to Wareham road, is now separated by parkland from both the Church of St. Andrew and Lulworth Castle but used to be clustered around the two buildings. The reasons for the village's decline and relocation are not clear, but it was perhaps yet another case of a local landowner extending his estate and improving his view.

The ancient manor house of East Lulworth was replaced in about 1600 by a hunting lodge in the style of a mock fortress, built by Thomas Howard, 3rd Viscount Bindon. In 1641 the property was sold to Humphrey Weld, which family still owns it today. It was substantially destroyed by fire in 1929 when Army personnel from the nearby camps joined fire-fighters in rescuing the family's belongings. In a reversal of fortune, the smoke-blackened ruin was abandoned and the adjacent small manor built.

Behind the castle is the Roman Catholic Church of St. Mary, looking like a domed garden house. Built in the 1780s following special permission granted by King George III, it was the first Roman Catholic church built in England after the Reformation. It was stipulated that although the building could go ahead, its purpose should not be obvious. The church has a beautiful interior which you should not miss.

St. Andrew's Church, East Lulworth, viewed from the top of Lulworth Castle.

Restoration of the castle by English Heritage is now complete. The castle is open every day except Christmas Day and there is an entrance charge. The towers provide superb views of the coast. The tea-room and small shop with unusual and inexpensive gifts are open to all. (Further information 01929-400510.)

TYNEHAM (3)

This is a recent desertion and one which remains controversial. The village is in the area of the Army firing ranges between Lulworth Cove and Kimmeridge, an outstandingly beautiful stretch of the Dorset coast. To the north, on the far side of Whiteway Hill, the tanks of Bovington have turned heath to desolate wasteland under their tracks. The area is closed to the public for much of the year, but at weekends and during school holidays there is usually access to Tyneham and to a network of glorious coastal walks. You can park at the top of Whiteway Hill and walk down, or there are car parks adjacent to Tyneham village.

In 1943 the inhabitants, many of which families had lived there for centuries, were persuaded to move out and allow the Army fuller access for essential battle training. The blow of their departure was softened with the promise of a speedy return after the war. It was a promise never kept. The village fell slowly into decay, with the tiny Church of St. Mary holding a very occasional service as though in defiance of fate. There is an exhibition in the old school putting the Ministry of Defence's case for continuing occupation and conservation of the surrounding countryside.

Walk from Tyneham down to Worbarrow Bay where more cottages used to stand, their occupants earning a living by fishing. Enjoy the peace, before perhaps driving inland to the Tank Museum at Bovington for a look at "Little Willie", the tank that started it all in 1915.

The Inland Tour

MILTON ABBAS (4)

One of the most picturesque in Dorset, this model village resulted from one man's desire to improve his view: Joseph Damer, later to become Baron Milton and Earl of Dorchester. Even as early as Domesday this was a large market town, centred on its abbey and renowned for its school endowed by one of the Abbots. After the Dissolution of the Monasteries, the whole was bought in 1540 by Sir John Tregonwell for £1,000. He took the Abbot's lodging as his own house.

The Tregonwells managed the estate for nearly two centuries, during which time a five year old son made history by falling twenty metres from the tower of the church and surviving. His ballooning petticoats softened his fall. One of the Tregonwells made provision in his will for an almshouse, which was built about 1674. When the new village was laid out a century later, the almshouse was moved and can still be seen today.

Joseph Damer bought the estate in 1752 and immediately began major and controversial changes. The Abbey Church of St. Mary, St. Samson and St. Branwalader, built after a fire in 1309 destroyed an older building, was retained, but the rest of the monastery was used to provide stone for a new house. The old Abbot's lodging was demolished, but the Great Hall of 1498 was incorporated into Damer's own seat, Milton Abbey House. North and west fronts of Portland stone, this impressive mansion faced onto parkland which was to be landscaped by "Capability" Brown.

Unfortunately the old houses of Milton Abbas spoiled the view so they, too, were demolished. A new village was built well away from the mansion and abbey, tucked into a narrow valley which provides beautiful surroundings. Built about 1780, the cob-walled, thatched cottages were each meant to house two families.

St. Catherine's chapel is perched at the head of a flight of grass steps on a nearby hill. It has Norman doors, windows and chancel arch, plus some interesting decorative floor tiles.

Milton Abbey House is now a school which, with the adjacent Abbey, enjoys one of the most spectacular sites in Dorset.

EASTBURY (5)

Only the gateway to a once magnificent house marks the location of this village just south of Tarrant Gunville. Eastbury House, designed by the great architect Vanbrugh, was built in 1738 for George Bubb Doddington who was to become Lord

Melcombe. It was of such immense proportions that when the owner died in 1762, neither a tenant nor a buyer could be found. Thirty years later the bulk of the building was demolished, partly by explosives, leaving only one stable wing and the gatehouse. The formal 17th century style gardens with parterre and canal were surrounded by parkland, providing a suitable setting for Vanbrugh's design.

The village of Eastbury stood near the main entrance to the house and part still remained in the early 19th century either side of the River Tarrant, since when it has completely disappeared. The reduced Eastbury House was occupied at the beginning of the 19th century by Thomas Wedgwood, whose father was the noted potter. There is a memorial to him in the village church.

To catch a glimpse of the house which is in private ownership, park carefully in Tarrant Gunville and walk up a small lane almost opposite the church, signposted as a footpath to Chettle. Follow the path past a small group of garages on your left and then along the back of gardens until you reach a small copse and kissing gate. Once through the gate a lovely walk along an avenue of beech trees skirts Eastbury House and its grounds to your right.

If you are lucky enough to be in the area in June when the village holds its fete in the gardens of Eastbury House, why not take the opportunity to join in the fun and see the house at closer quarters?

KNOWLTON (6)

Knowlton church.

A Christian church in the centre of a Neolithic earthwork stands to the west of the B3078 from Wimborne Minster to Cranborne. The ruin is of a 12th century building, enlarged in the 15th century when the village was of significant size, stretching along the south-east bank of the River Allen about 500 metres away.

By 1659 the church must have seen dwindling congregations because it was suggested that the building be demolished. Permission was refused and it wasn't until the roof collapsed in the early 18th century that it was completely abandoned.

The area is rich in prehistoric monuments. Knowlton Circles are four enclosures which "represent the remains of a ritual or ceremonial centre of the late Neolithic period" (Royal Commission on Historical Monuments). Nearby are forty-two round barrows, their concentration indicating that this was a site of considerable importance from the earliest of times.

WINTERBORNE TOMSON (7)

A delightful church, a 17th century house and a large farm are all that are left of the old village to the north of the Wimborne Minster to Dorchester road. The church is of 12th century origin, with enclosed pews and a small gallery. It was restored in 1930 by A.R. Powys, financed by the sale of letters written by Dorset author Thomas Hardy to the Society for the Protection of Ancient Buildings, a subject which was always close to his heart.

Reynolds Stone, an artist and wood engraver from Litton Cheney, carved the commemorative plaque from Purbeck marble.

OF HISTORICAL INTEREST

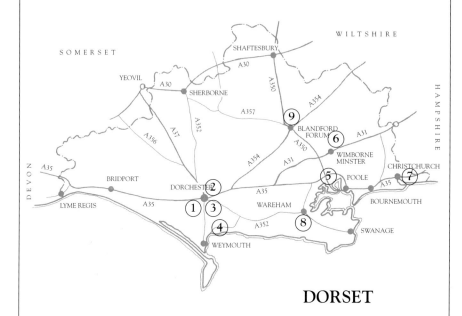

DORSET

THE ROMAN TOUR
1. Maiden Castle
2. Dorchester's Roman Town House and Walks
3. Maumbury Rings
4. Bowleaze Temple, Preston
5. Romano-British Farmstead, Upton Country Park

THE NORMAN TOUR
6. Wimborne Minster
7. Constable's House, Christchurch
8. Corfe Castle

THE GEORGIAN TOUR
9. A walk around Blandford Forum

OF HISTORICAL INTEREST

The different ages of Dorset man can be traced from prehistory to the present day through buildings and other structures - standing stones to hillforts, humble cottages to lofty cathedrals. This chapter describes three tours, each of which will bring you into contact with an era which has stamped its mark firmly on the face of the county.

The Romans arrived in Dorset in 43 AD, storming Maiden Castle and overthrowing the Durotriges who inhabited the area. The banks of the nearby River Frome provided a level site for a new town and the first timber houses were soon erected in what we now know as Dorchester, the county town that has its feet firmly in Roman sandals. The position of the surrounding Roman walls is still marked by shady promenades known as the Walks where, on a misty night, you might still imagine you hear the change of guard across the centuries. It is an ideal central position from which to explore Dorset's Roman heritage, driving out to find arrow-straight roads along which the Legions marched.

Ask any schoolboy what happened in 1066 and it is pretty certain he will answer: "The Battle of Hastings". King Harold, defeated and with an arrow in the eye for good measure, fell before the Norman Conquest. The invaders soon became settlers, building churches in unmistakable style; none so fine as at Studland on a small scale, and at Wimborne Minster. The most atmospheric ruin of all, Corfe Castle, stands as an example of their fortifications.

In quite a different style the Georgians left us an inheritance of elegant buildings, paned and sashed windows, moulded door casings and a definite air of gentility. Many fires ravaged Dorset's towns over the centuries, consuming tightly-packed thatched cottages and timber-framed dwellings so that rebuilding in stone and brick in the Georgian era was as much necessity as conceit. Examples are everywhere, but Blandford Forum is a showcase for this style of architecture.

Romans, Normans, Georgians; Saxon burials, Tudor manors, Victorian industrial buildings; all rub shoulders with 20th century architecture and make Dorset a county worth exploring.

The Roman Tour

MAIDEN CASTLE (1)

Six thousand years ago Neolithic tribesmen built a primitive camp, a rough circle of ditches enclosing a bank, within the perimeter of what is now Maiden Castle. The purpose is unclear and could have been ceremonial, but it is generally agreed that the camp was not a settlement. A century or so later the longest Neolithic barrow known was constructed through the centre, just over 540 metres from end to end. While other such barrows were used for burials, this was not the case here and the barrow remains shrouded in mystery. However within sight of Maiden Castle, particularly along the Ridgeway above Weymouth, there are an amazing number of barrows indicating that the whole area had great importance in those early times.

At some stage Maiden Castle was abandoned but grew to prominence again in the Iron Age, about 600 BC, when it was gradually increased in size and fortified as the tribal centre of the Durotriges, a name that has been handed down from the Romans. This expansion into one of the country's most impressive hillforts took over four hundred years, at a time when other such earthworks were being built at Eggardon, Hambledon and Hod, amongst others. Poundbury, on the north-west corner of Dorchester, is of similar date but never became the massive enclosure that the other hillforts exemplify.

The Romans invaded in 43 AD, the method of their victory indicated in the War Cemetery excavated on Maiden Castle by Sir Mortimer Wheeler in the 1930s. The defenders, it is believed, hurled rounded pebbles collected from Chesil Beach at their attackers through sling-shot, but to no avail. One skeleton of the three dozen or so uncovered had a Roman arrow-head through the spine. This and other artefacts are now in the Dorset County Museum, which sets out the history of the area in interesting and imaginative displays.

The hillfort gave the Durotriges commanding views of the surrounding countryside, views which today remain unhindered by development except for Dorchester, the Roman town of Durnovaria, which was under construction an estimated twenty years after the invasion.

In the 4th century the Romans added a temple to the slopes of the hillfort, the footings of which can still be seen. A second temple has been found at Jordan Hill, Bowleaze, overlooking Weymouth Bay (see 4).

TOWN HOUSE AND THE WALKS, DORCHESTER (2)

It did not take the Romans long to plan their new town called Durnovaria. The remains of timber buildings dated close to 60 AD prove that the site was settled soon after the invasion. About a century later the growing town was encircled by a ditch and bank, the latter being topped by a stone wall in the 4th century.

In the 1930s, when Colliton Park had been bought by Dorset County Council as a site for their new County Hall, excavations brought to light a Roman town house. (This has been the pattern of subsequent excavations in Dorchester, when new development invariably uncovers Roman remains. The long-stay car park behind Agriculture House in Acland Road is sited over the Roman baths.) Once the footings had been uncovered, spacious rooms with mosaic floors became evident. An underfloor heating system was supplied to some rooms and stone pillars found down a nearby well indicate an elegant colonnade.

Surviving remnant of the Roman wall.

Roman Town House, Dorchester.

The house is now displayed in a manner that befits its importance. Future intentions for the site include an information centre on the town's Roman heritage. The house lies to the north of County Hall and can be reached from Top o' Town, along Colliton Walk which runs behind Hardy's statue and then high above The Grove, then turning right into North Walk. The gate into the town house site is a little way along on the right hand side. The Walks lie on top of the Roman defensive banks, The Grove clearly indicating the depth of the encircling ditch.

Also at Top o' Town, just inside Albert Road, is the only remaining section of Roman wall, a small panel which is undoubtedly part of the oldest stone "building" in Dorchester. From here you can follow West Walks, running south past the Borough Gardens; turn left at the end into Bowling Alley Walk; cross Trinity Street and South Street into South Walks Road. At the Martyrs statues, cross Icen Way then turn left into Salisbury Fields and you are still following the line of the Roman walls. You will emerge where Fordington High Street joins High East Street, at the lower end of town.

MAUMBURY RINGS (3)

Adjacent to Dorchester South railway station, Maumbury Rings is a large, grassy enclosure which remained anonymous until Sir Christopher Wren, the great architect of St. Paul's Cathedral, passed by. On his way to Portland to buy stone, he identified it as a Roman amphitheatre. Since then the site has yielded other secrets.

Like Maiden Castle, the Rings has its origins in Neolithic times, dug out with antler picks some of which have been found on site. The Romans made use of its potential by raising the bank to enclose displays of wild animals and possibly gladiatorial combat. In the 17th century Civil War fortifications were placed here, Dorchester being staunchly Parliamentarian. It was a token gesture of resistance. The town surrendered to the Royalists the following year when the first war-like threats were made, discretion obviously being the better part of valour.

Maumbury Rings was often used for large patriotic gatherings. The grassy slopes, which have held up to ten thousand people, also provided good viewing for public executions and at one time the gallows were sited here. These remain shadows of the past when, on a sunny, summer's evening, Dorchester people once again crowd the slopes to enjoy outdoor theatre or a celebration of May time.

TEMPLE, BOWLEAZE (4)

The remains of a small building thought to have been a Roman temple, or at least used for some ritual purpose, were excavated at Bowleaze close to the River

Jordan in 1843. Situated on a small hill at the northern end of Weymouth Bay behind Bowleaze Cove, the view is beautiful despite being dominated to the east by a holiday complex.

A Tuscan capital in Purbeck marble was uncovered nearby, scaled to top a column of about 1.6 metres high. A deep shaft within the building contained bird bones and those of a hare. There was apparently a larger, surrounding enclosure, in which were found ox horns, pottery and 4th century coins. Thirty years earlier a hoard of silver coins had been discovered on the hill, and in 1928 a huge cache of over four and a half thousand bronze coins came to light.

The finds, including the posts of what were thought to be a Roman landing stage in the cove itself, suggest occupation from the early years of the Romans. A burial on the cliffs included a gold ring and a bronze battleaxe.

There is now little to see except the site with remnants of the stone footings, but it has yielded much of interest and who knows, may still hold some surprises.

ROMANO-BRITISH HOMESTEAD, UPTON (5)

Upton Country Park on the outskirts of Poole has a full-scale reconstruction of the type of homestead that would have been found in the area from 43AD onwards, when the pottery and salt making industries first got under way.

It is the result of painstaking research and a determination to use the methods and tools of the time. Ancient pollen grains preserved in the ground were analysed to find out what kind of trees would have been growing in the area, and hence what sort of wood could have been used for building. Fascinating!

The homestead is always on view but is also used for specific projects throughout the year, encouraging children to take part as they learn about their ancestors.

The country park is open every day and admission is free unless a special event is being held. Further information from 01202-672628.

The Norman Tour

WIMBORNE MINSTER (6)

The town was founded in the early 8th century with two monasteries and had developed into a small market town by the time of the Norman Conquest in 1066. The minster church was built by the Normans and dedicated to St. Cuthberga. It is a striking, twin-towered building built of stone in two different colours, russet and cream.

Apart from the building itself, the minster is full of interest. The chained library is rare and dates from 1686. The west tower clock features the "Quarter

Norman Arcading, Christchurch Priory.

The Norman House, Christchurch.

Jack", a small figure in Napoleonic uniform who comes out to strike the quarter hours, and the main tower has as astronomical clock with revolving planets.

There is also the tomb of Anthony Ettrick, "the man in the wall". He vowed to be buried neither in the church nor in churchyard, so his sarcophagus was inserted in the thickness of the wall. He predicted his date of death as 1691 and even went so far as to have that date pre-carved on his tomb. It had to be altered since he lived a further twelve years.

CONSTABLE'S HOUSE, CHRISTCHURCH (7)

The town sits between the rivers Stour and Avon and is dominated by the Priory, the longest parish church in England.

A 13th century castle was constructed here by Baldwin de Redvers and the nearby Constable's House is believed to have been the hall of that castle. Both are now ruined but their siting, with the house on the mill stream bank, is well worth a visit. All that is left of the castle are two walls of the keep. The house, one of the oldest in England, was built of Purbeck marble in rough blocks. The surviving masonry includes a chimney and garderobe (lavatory) tower.

You can't visit Christchurch and not look at the Priory, also substantially

Norman. The outside of the north transept in particular has unmistakable Norman arched decoration. Inside, don't miss the "miraculous beam" which, cut too short during building operations, was found the next day to be the right length and in position.

On leaving Christchurch there are two options. There is an inland route, a fast road across the north of Bournemouth and Poole, then bypass Wareham to Corfe Castle.

The more scenic route is to head for Sandbanks at Poole and cross the harbour mouth on the ferry to Studland, thence to Corfe Castle.

CORFE CASTLE (8)

The castle and village are a delight and attract visitors at all times of year. Parking is therefore at a premium but there is a large National Trust car park off the approach road from Wareham. The closely-packed village is dominated by the spectacular ruins of the castle, built on top of a high mound to guard the entrance into the Isle of Purbeck.

Corfe Castle.

This is not really an island, but certainly the character of this part of Dorset sets it distinctly apart from the rest of the county. It is an area where dinosaurs roamed, where myths and legends are many.

The castle site was bought by William the Conqueror who erected the inner bailey at the top of the mound and enclosed this with a defensive wall. Over two centuries the castle expanded, additional buildings taking shape until, eventually, the hill was surrounded at its base by another wall. The castle was used as a Royal seat, a base for hunting in Purbeck, but became a more domestic dwelling in the 16th century.

In 1635 in was bought by the Bankes family and it is Lady Bankes who has gone down in history as the heroine of the castle. In 1643 it was besieged by Parliamentarians in the Civil War but Lady Bankes, with only a garrison of five men and a handful of women servants, held fast against them. Three years later the castle was under siege again and Parliamentary troops were able to enter the stronghold, Lady Bankes having been betrayed by one of her garrison.

The building was blown up with gunpowder but the core of the building stood firm - albeit at some strange angles. The ruins have tumbled picturesquely down the hill ever since.

The Georgian Tour

A WALK AROUND BLANDFORD FORUM (9)

Timber and thatch, cob and thatch, make picturesque cottages, but when fire breaks out it spreads with incredible speed. Blandford Forum, like other Dorset towns, suffered a series of fires through the centuries, but in 1731 came a fire that was awful in its severity. It started in a tallow chandler's shop on the site of the King's Arms and, in no time at all, three quarters of the town was destroyed and thousands made homeless.

So great was the devastation that a co-ordinated rebuilding programme was planned under the eyes of brothers John and William Bastard. They were designers, surveyors, builders, all in one, and it is thanks to their overall involvement that the town presents such a perfect Georgian appearance today. Mellow brick, white-painted windows, rubbed brick arches and decorative cornices are topped by steep tiled roofs. Details may vary but there is an overall conformity of proportions, materials and scale.

The town centres around the Market Place with the Parish Church of St. Peter and St. Paul in a prominent position. The Bastard family are commemorated by an obelisk in the churchyard and the nearby Town Pump was erected by the brothers as a monument to the great fire. The church was altered internally in 1895, but the stone exterior is pure Georgian.

Walk a little way along East Street to find Stour House on the right and Lyston House on the left, both splendid examples of the rebuilding which was

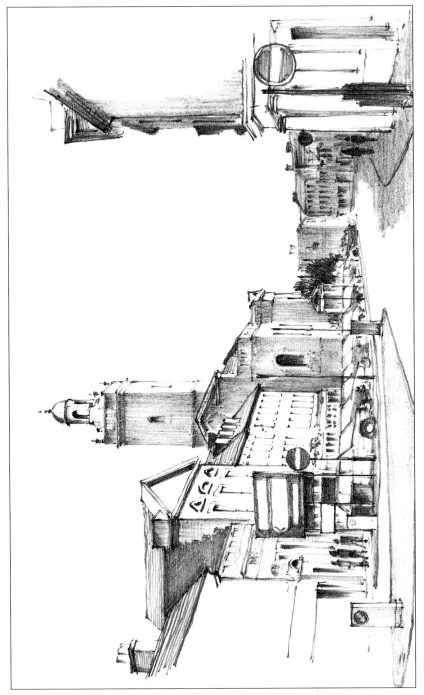

View of the Market Place and the Church of St. Peter & St. Paul, Blandford Forum.

mostly in red brick. This was almost the extent of the fire in this direction, rebuilding after a previous fire resulting in tiled roofs in this area which were protection against later damage. Eastway House, a little further along on the right, was an exception and now has a lovely Georgian frontage complete with imposing door, decorative urns and front railings.

Turn back towards the church and follow the narrow alley on your right, Tabernacle Walk, which leads through to The Close. Turn left and immediately on your left is the Old House, which survived the fire. It was built in the mid-17th century by a German, Dr. Sagittary, who perhaps expressed the character of his native country in the rusticated brickwork, heavy roof and tall chimney stacks. This solid building makes a good comparison with the finer elements of Georgian architecture which surround it. As you reach the wider space of The Tabernacle, immediately ahead is a stone commemorating the tercentenary of the granting of the Royal Charter in 1605.

Bear left down Sheep Market Hill, keeping your eyes open for the headless sheep that reputedly haunts the area. As long as you are not wandering the streets at midnight, you should be safe from this apparition! Turn right along the north of the churchyard and note the old entrance in the garden wall which used to lead to the church almshouses, now sadly demolished.

Turn right again, up Church Lane to The Plocks where sheep were herded ready for market. Coupar House, at the top of Church Lane on the right, has a grand facade with stone dressings and decorative details. Lime Tree House opposite is classically Georgian and a beautiful example of its kind.

Turning left, walk through to Salisbury Street. A right turn will bring you to Ryves Almshouses. These are some of Blandford's older buildings, dating from 1682, and were built to provide shelter for "ten impecunious persons" who paid 2/6d (12.5p) a week, which included the use of a grey gown.

Walk back the way you have come and read the plaque on no: 38 Salisbury Street. Alfred Stevens, born here in 1818, was a famous Victorian sculptor and painter and is best known for his monument to the Duke of Wellington in St. Paul's Cathedral. Examples of his work can be seen in Chettle House, on the Salisbury Road out of Blandford.

Continue past the entrance to The Plocks, to the junction of Whitecliff Mill Street on the right hand side. Note the early date on the fascia of one building there. This must have been one of the first buildings to catch fire in 1731, since it was so near the seat of the blaze. Over on the left is the entrance to the old Anchor Inn under an original oriel window. The brackets were for fire ladders. A little further down on the same side, above the shop with the bow window, is an example of mathematical tiling, a facing of tile slips hung on timber to resemble brick.

As Salisbury Street reaches the Market Place the view east to the church opens up. Facing this view are more excellent examples of Georgian building, although the Crown Hotel is a modern rebuilding of that style following its destruction by a lorry. The keystones over the windows were retained and the facade constructed to resemble the original 'header' bricks, when the smaller end of the brick faces outwards rather than the longer side.

Make your way back through the Market Place which contains the best of what the Bastards had to offer. Greyhound House, the old Greyhound Inn, has a superb stucco frontage with elaborate window surrounds, bunches of grapes decoration and Corinthian capitalled pillars. The Red Lion Inn also boasts pillars with impressive capitals. On the corner of Bere's Yard is the Bastard's own home. More decorative capitals and a rampant lion over the upper arched window make this an imposing house. On the north side of the Market Place is the Corn Exchange, another facade of stone, with a triple-arched entrance and lantern lights.

Blandford Museum is tucked away inside Bere's Yard and makes an excellent way to round off your visit to the town. It is open every day in summer and there is a small entrance charge.

INDUSTRIAL DORSET

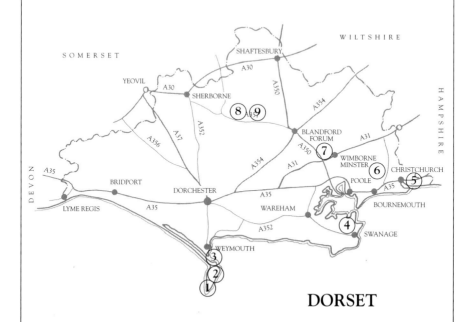

DORSET

THE STONE TOUR
1. Portland Museum
2. The quarries
3. The breakwater
4. Men of stone, Swanage

THE MILLS TOUR
5. Place Mill, Christchurch
6. Throop Mill, Bournemouth
7. White Mill, Sturminster Marshall
8. Sturminster Mill, Sturminster Newton
9. Fiddleford Mill

INDUSTRIAL DORSET

Dorset has thankfully remained a rural county, which is what makes it so attractive to visitors. No great factory chimneys massed together, no sooty towns, no waste lands of industrial debris creating eyesores.

How, then, have people made their living over the centuries? Farming has been a way of life for many, the chalk downs supporting vast flocks of sheep. Flax and hemp flourished in the fields, giving rise to rope making and netting that are still continued in Bridport. Fleets of small boats fished coastal waters while, from Poole in particular, larger vessels made money for their owners by undertaking the hazardous voyage to the Newfoundland fishing grounds.

Cottage industries included the making of gloves and shoes, and the unique hand-made Dorset buttons. Poole pottery, now eminently collectable as well as for current use, is still produced and shipped all over the world. Brickworks flourished, with local building materials coming from Swanage, Chickerell, and Broadmayne to name just a few.

There were many mills, mostly for grain but some for paper production. These were powered by the swift-flowing rivers and even the smallest of water-courses had its share. Dorset's most enduring industry, however, is the quarrying of stone: Purbeck stone, for the sturdy cottages on the Isle of Purbeck and beyond; Portland stone, used not only in this county but extensively in London's great buildings and worldwide.

While the cottage industries have disappeared virtually without trace, milling and stone provide two fascinating insights into Dorset's industrial heritage.

The Stone Tour

PORTLAND MUSEUM (1)

It makes sense to visit the Portland Museum before beginning to explore the island further. It was Dr. Marie Stopes, pioneer of birth control, who in 1930 founded this informative little museum off Wakeham, just above Church Ope Cove. She was its first curator.

The Portland Gallery tells the story of the island and its famous stone industry as well as giving information about the Verne prison. Shipwrecks and smuggling feature in Marie Stopes Cottage, another section of the museum, while children will enjoy the dinosaur pit and the World War II bomb which, when uncovered in 1995, led to mass evacuation of the island until the mechanism was rendered harmless.

The museum is open from Easter to October from 10.30 a.m. to 5 p.m., except Wednesdays and Thursdays. It is closed for half an hour from 1 p.m. for lunch. Check opening times and admission charge on 01305-821804.

THE QUARRIES, PORTLAND (2)

Drive back to the Portland Heights Hotel overlooking the harbour and Chesil

Beach and park where indicated, to the right hand side of the main road. Walk back across the main road and follow the paths that lead in to Tout's Quarry and the sculpture park. Here you are free to roam in what used to be one of the island's working quarries. The spoil was transported by carts to the cliffs where it could be tipped over the edge.

In early years the quarried stone was loaded and taken to the docks in horsedrawn wagons, a precarious business since the paths down to sea-level were steep and often slippery. Later a train was used and the old railway tracks can still be seen.

One of the unusual features of Tout's Quarry is the sculpture. Some are easily found, but others are tucked away in unlikely corners. Each year, it seems, an extra fantasy is added or an old one disappears.

On the other side of the main road, closer to the car parks, you can follow the footpaths round more old quarry workings now becoming covered in vegetation. This trail leads past a working quarry where care must be taken not to obstruct the lorries bringing out the stone. You may find the Victorian gun emplacement tucked in on the top of the headland and you will clearly see the route of the railway passing under the stone bridges on its way to the quays.

THE BREAKWATER (3)

The enduring qualities of Portland stone can be appreciated in the breakwater that protects the harbour. The Prince Consort laid the foundation stone in 1849, the rest being transported and laid by convict labour - who had first to build their own accommodation. There is a 314 metre section with a fort at its northern end, and a 1846 metre section with the "Palmerston's Folly" of the Nothe Fort on the Weymouth shore. Both were completed in 1872.

MEN OF STONE (4)

Moving from the Isle of Portland to the Isle of Purbeck, notice the traditional cottages in Purbeck stone. Very different, this, from creamy Portland stone which was usually laid in regular blocks. Here the limestone is darker and rougher in texture. Not only is it used for walls, but stone tiles are laid as roofing material. The cottages look as though they could withstand any gale with such a weight keeping them firmly on the ground. A good example is the picturesque village of Corfe Castle.

As you drive into Swanage, bricks from the local works become more in evidence. It was here that John Mowlem was born in 1788, son of a local quarryman. By 1823 he had established his own firm, using Purbeck limestone to pave roads in the capital and shipping it from Swanage to a wharf in Pimlico. Twelve years later he was joined by another Swanage man, George Burt, and the two prospered.

Mowlem bought Herston House in Swanage in 1849. All that now remains is a stone tablet set into a garden wall in the High Street with the simple inscription:

Through route to Merchant's Railway for quarried stone.

Purbeck stone roof.

J.M.1850. He also erected the granite column on the sea front, to commemorate a battle between King Alfred and the Danes in Swanage Bay in AD 877 (although it is questioned whether such a battle ever really took place).

When Mowlem retired, George Burt, his nephew by marriage, kept the firm going. His increasing prosperity meant he could enhance Swanage with his love of stone and he soon became known as the King of Swanage. He built Purbeck House in the High Street, bringing items from London to create his ideal home. The archway came from Grosvenor Place; one of the statues came from Billingsgate Market; pieces of moulded stone and floor tiles came from the Palace of Westminster.

Burt also built the Town Hall, the frontage of which had been rescued from London's Mercers' Hall demolished in 1860-61. See if you can find the London lamp standards along the Parade and Beach Road, inscribed "St. George Hanover Square" and "City of London". The fanciful Wellington Tower on Peveril Point came from Southwark.

One of Burt's outstanding contributions to the area was Durlston Castle high above Peveril Point. This is now surrounded by the Country Park and is a lovely place to walk. Three granite posts which give heights above sea level were originally destined for Trafalgar Square. The Great Globe of Portland stone was made in Mowlem's Greenwich works and transported to Swanage in fifteen segments.

No wonder this became known as London-by-the-Sea!

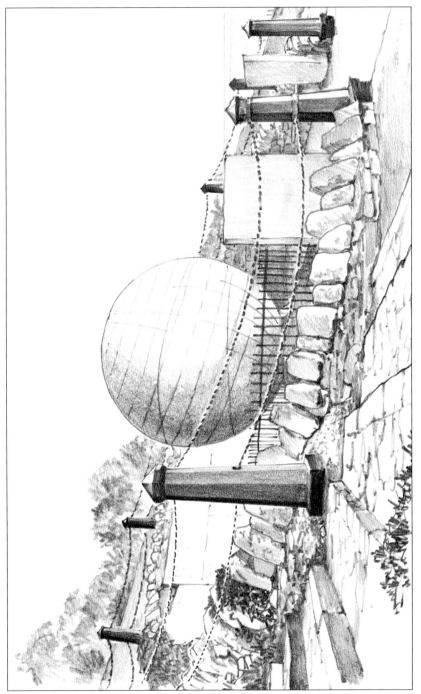

The Swanage Globe, of Portland Stone.

The Mills Tour

PLACE MILL, CHRISTCHURCH (5)

Place Mill on Christchurch Quay was unique in being driven by the tides. The mill is listed in the Domesday Book as the Corn Mill of the Canons of Holy Trinity, Twynham, this being the old name for Christchurch. Damaged severely by fire in 1400, it was rebuilt and then enlarged in the 16th century. Once owned by Henry

Place Mill, Christchurch.

Prince of Wales, son of James I, and then by Charles I, the mill was bought at auction in 1888 by Christchurch Borough Council who bid £1,000 for the historic building.

The last miller left in 1908 and the mill lay quiet until restored and opened in 1983. It is opened to the public on Sunday afternoons by the local trust who now manage its affairs. There is a small shop.

THROOP MILL, BOURNEMOUTH (6)

Just south of Hurn Airport is the village of Throop, reached from the A3060 Christchurch to Kinson road. The mill is a large, imposing building rebuilt in 1912, although like most of the mills in Dorset there has been a building on this site for nearly nine centuries.

White Mill, Sturminster Marshall.

The name on the side is Parsons & Sons, who bought the mill and ground flour there from 1926 onwards, the machinery powered by a water turbine. In 1972 the River Stour was diverted and the mill building became redundant. Walk past the mill towards Mill Road and take the left hand path signed to West Hurn. This will take you across the river sluices, some of which were made by Dorset Iron Foundry Co. of Poole and some by Lott & Walne of Dorchester.

Look out for Throop Mill Cottage on the old river line, its thatched roof making it arguably the prettiest building in Bournemouth.

WHITE MILL, STURMINSTER MARSHALL (6)

Sturminster Marshall's lovely old bridge over the Stour is worth visiting on its own, but the restoration of the adjacent White Mill by the National Trust makes it doubly interesting. Entry is free to NT members but there is an admission charge for others.

The mill was one of eight in the Wimborne area on the River Stour and once kept close company with a second mill on this site, one milling grain and the other processing woollen cloth. The fall of the river is insufficient on its own to drive a mill wheel, the surrounding farmland being very flat, and several weirs were constructed up-stream to direct sufficient head of water through the mill race. The site had another drawback - at times of heavy rain and increased river level, the mill flooded as the river burst its banks.

The mill underwent substantial rebuilding by the Bankes Estate in the mid-18th century and was then let to John Joyce for £20 a year. The Joyce family worked the mill from 1776 until it finally closed in 1906. The dilapidation of the weir system hastened its demise. H. S. Joyce, whose father was the last miller, gave an insight into life in the mill in a book called: "I was born in the country".

Two sets of machinery survive with parts carved from elm and applewood, probably of 18th century origin, and the stones are of French Burr and Derbyshire Grit. The mill produced high-quality flour and, in the lean-to bakehouses, bread and cakes.

There is a car park close to the mill but care must be taken crossing the road. The old stone bridge with its cut-waters and refuges is narrow and traffic passes one way at a time. The River Stour is broad and beautiful, with a walk along its banks.

STURMINSTER MILL, STURMINSTER NEWTON (7)

The setting of this Grade II Listed mill could not be more perfect. At Domesday there were four mills listed on the River Stour at Sturminster Newton, although this one was restored and enlarged in the 17th century. The nearby six-arch bridge, built in the 16th century, gives a splendid view as cars wait to take their turn on the single lane system, crossing from tiny Newton into the larger market town of Sturminster.

In 1775 great festivities were held around a bonfire built on the site of the weir pool, which had been drained. The firing of cannon and an excellent band of music made it a noisy occasion.

At the beginning of this century the millstones were replaced by steel hammers and the water wheel replaced by an undershot water turbine made not too far away, in Ringwood. The mill is still operated and open to the public from time to time, with a small admission charge. You can inspect all three floors, guided by members of the Sturminster Mill Museum Society.

FIDDLEFORD MILL (9)

Between Sturminster Newton and Hammoon a public footpath takes you across the sluices of Fiddleford Mill, parts of which date from the 14th and 15th centuries. A two-column text inscription with the date of 1566 can be seen on one of the buildings. It is weather-worn and difficult to read, but translates as:

OPERAM DEDI

He that wyll have any thynge don

A frynd to the owner and enemy to no man

In the tale of trothe I do allway professe

Appere the fault shalbe thyne

Therefore to be true yt shall these behove

MEIS SUMPIS ALIENIS

Let him com fryndly he shalbe welcom

Freely to com when they can

Myller be true Disgrace no thy vest

Sharp punishment think me not unkind

To please God chiefly that liveth above.

It is hoped that English Heritage will eventually restore Fiddleford Mill to working order. The nearby manor house is one of the earliest in Dorset and is open to the public.

STRANGE BUT TRUE

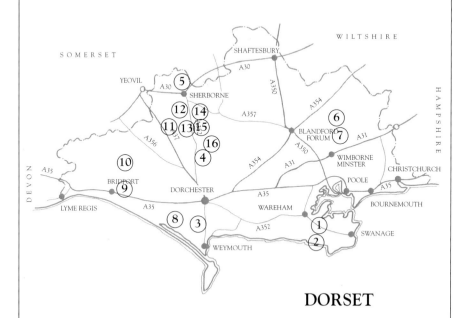

DORSET

THE FOLLIES AND FANCIES TOUR

1. Creech Arch, West Creech
2. Clavel Tower, Kimmeridge
3. Spa House, Nottington
4. Smith's Arms, Godmanstone
5. The Conduit, Sherborne
6. Horton Tower
7. Cottage orné, Stanbridge

THE CURIOSITIES TOUR

8. The undecided worshipper, Portesham
9. King Charles II's escape route
10. Posy Tree, Mapperton
11. The tiny church, Stockwood
12. Cross-in-Hand, Batcombe
13. The miller's gravestone, Sydling
14. The oldest PO box in use, Holywell
15. Cerne Abbas Giant
16. St. Augustine's Well, Cerne Abbas

STRANGE BUT TRUE

There is so much in Dorset that we take for granted. Things we see every day that have become so much a part of the landscape that we fail to look properly, asking how and why. These oddities - be they man-made or natural - are threads of the county's rich historical tapestry.

It is fun searching them out, exploring more fully. They each tell a story about a place, a person or an event, that is strange - but true.

The Follies and Fancies Tour

CREECH ARCH, WEST CREECH (1)

This tour begins at Wareham where you take the A351 to Corfe Castle. Branch right at Stoborough through Creech and then past Creech Grange on the right. Glimpses of the fine stone house can be had from the drive up onto the ridge. Once past the Grange continue up the hill to a car park at the top. A track from here leads east to the folly.

Creech Folly was built in the 18th century to improve the view from the Grange, owned by the Bond family who were extensive landowners and who gave their name to London's Bond Street. It is a romantic stretch of wall broken by archways and decorated with small pinnacles. Apart from seeking out the folly from curiosity, this is some of the finest walking the county has to offer. The Purbeck ridge coupled with wide tracts of land now owned by the National Trust ensure that this area just inland from the sea is every bit as picturesque as the dramatic coastline itself.

CLAVEL TOWER, KIMMERIDGE (2)

Almost due south of Creech Arch, right on the coast, is the Clavel Tower. Otherwise known as the Kimmeridge Folly, this circular building that looks rather like a chess piece occupies a dramatic position overlooking Kimmeridge Bay. It is a steep pull up from the beach. The tower is now in poor condition but the view is worth the effort.

The folly was built by the Reverend John Richards who, in 1817, had inherited the Smedmore Estate and taken the name of Clavel. The building dates from 1831.

THE HOUSE BUILT ON WATER (3)

The Spa House, Nottington, mid-way between Weymouth and Dorchester, is now privately owned. It is a pretty, octagonal building with three storeys, in which the basement still houses the machinery to pump water from the spring over which it is built. It is not open to the public.

In the mid-17th century, so we are led to believe, a flock of sheep was being driven past the spring and its pond. Many of them dipped in the water and, to the shepherd's surprise, were cured of various ailments. News of the health-giving

Spa House, Nottington.   Smith's Arms, Godmanstone.

properties of the water spread and soon people were arriving to try and find a cure for their own ills. In 1791 King George III brought his Queen and, as the crowds increased, it was decided a spa house should be built. The Spa House was opened in 1830.

SMITH'S ARMS, GODMANSTONE (4)

This is England's smallest pub. Landlord John Foster, an ex jockey, has fought hard to maintain the Smith's Arms' place in the Guinness Book of Records for its diminutive size. Small it might be, but it is crammed full of character. Its position on the bank of the River Cerne about 4 miles north of Dorchester adds to its charm and locals and holidaymakers alike enjoy stopping off for refreshment.

The smithy earned its place in history when King Charles II rode by and asked for a drink of ale. The smith replied that he had no licence to provide ale, only water. There and then the king licensed the premises and they have remained so ever since.

THE CONDUIT, SHERBORNE (5)

In the centre of Sherborne stands this robust 16th century building, once a monks' washhouse. After the Dissolution of the Monasteries it was moved here from the Abbey grounds and provided a water supply for the residents. Staunchly Royalist, when King Charles II regained the throne the town made festive use of the Conduit and it is said that it "ran with clarret besides many hogsheads of March Bear".

Dwarfing the Conduit is Sherborne's magnificent Abbey, with a most beautiful fan-vaulted roof.

HORTON TOWER (6)

Lying to the east of the B3078 Wimborne/Cranborne road is Horton Tower. Folly or observatory, the tower is a well-known landmark overlooking the Cranborne Chase. Built in 1726 by Humphrey Sturt, a local landowner, the strangely constructed red brick tower was once part of a large estate.

Horton Tower

The six-storey tower is basically hexagonal, with three-quarter round turrets added to the lower storeys every alternate face, giving the whole a more triangular appearance. The interior now is bare, the beam holes for the floor joists clearly visible, as is a fireplace now suspended halfway up.

Forty years after the tower was built, the family moved to nearby More Crichel and Horton Tower rapidly fell into disuse. It stands today to tantalise all who wonder why it was really built.

Take the road from Horton to Chalbury Common. Just before the Chalbury sign there is a lay-by on the right hand side where you can park with care. Opposite, a bridleway leads to the side of Tower House and five minutes will bring you to the tower and its wonderful viewpoint.

COTTAGE ORNÉ, STANBRIDGE (7)

On your way back towards Wimborne, if you take the B3078 you will pass the delightful cottage orné at Stanbridge. It is on a difficult corner and there are no pavements so, if you wish to photograph, park safely as soon as you can and retrace your steps to the house.

The highly decorative cottages orné were popular in Georgian times. They were often of unusual shape, with scalloped thatch and lead-paned windows. There are others in Dorset. One at Winterborne Came, just south of Dorchester, was the home of dialect poet and minister William Barnes. Umbrella Cottage at Lyme Regis has the most exteme design of thatch, as its name suggests. There is also a cottage orné in the old village centre at Wool.

Stanbridge, Cottage Orné.

Please remember that this is not open to the public; respect the occupier's privacy.

The Curiosities Tour

THE UNDECIDED WORSHIPPER (8)

William Weare died in 1670, leaving behind something of a puzzle. He did not wish to be buried inside Portesham church - nor outside. Since his remains had to be laid to rest somewhere, his wish was granted by placing his tomb within the church south wall, part in and part out, where it remains today. His epitaph begins: "William Weare lies here in dust/As thou and I and all men must ..."

Interestingly, Anthony Ettrick of Wimborne caused a similar furore a few years later. Neither inside the Minster, nor outside; neither above ground, nor below; his coffin was similarly placed in a specially formed recess in the Minster wall when he died in 1703.

Portesham is on the B3157 Weymouth/Bridport road. It was the home of Admiral Sir Thomas Masterman Hardy, who was with Lord Nelson when he died on board HMS Victory at the Battle of Trafalgar.

KING CHARLES II's ESCAPE ROUTE (9)

After his defeat at the Battle of Worcester in 1651, King Charles II headed first for

Bristol and then turned back into Dorset to try and make good his escape. He was hoping for a ship from Charmouth but, when this failed, rode further east to Bridport. The King had been spotted at Charmouth, however, and with a pursuing troop of Parliamentarians hard on his heels he decided to ride hard for Trent, in the north of the county, where he could hide in a priest's hole in the Manor House.

The King's party reached the eastern limits of Bridport and turned left up Lee Lane, still narrow and overhung by trees today and probably then little more than a trackway. One can imagine them perhaps holding their horses silent for the few minutes it took the Roundheads to gallop past along the Dorchester road. The King then continued north to safety and eventual escape.

A memorial carving which used to be on an old wall is now on the left hand side as you enter Lee Lane, sheltered appropriately by an oak tree. "When midst your fiercest foes on every side/For your escape God did a lane provide."

THE POSY TREE (10)

Take the B3163 out of Beaminster towards the A356 and Dorchester, watching for the turning right and the brown tourist sign to Mapperton gardens. Follow that narrower road past the entrance to Mapperton and continue for about half a mile when, on your right, you will see the remains of the Posy Tree.

Posy Tree, Mapperton.

The notice indicates that it was past this tree that victims of the Great Plague were carried to a common grave by the survivors. An earlier sign is believed to have stated that posies of wild herbs and flowers were collected here en route to the burial place, in the hopes of averting the spread of the disease.

This claim has now been challenged, since it was apparently in the earlier plague of 1582 that around eighty inhabitants of Mapperton died. It was then the custom to bury the village dead in Netherbury churchyard but, because of fear of the disease, Netherbury people gathered at the Posy Tree armed with staves to prevent the infected bodies from passing into their parish.

Whatever the story the remains of the Posy Tree recall a time when death struck with frightening speed, bringing devastation to many families and completely wiping out others. It is a grim reminder, beautiful though this old sycamore must once have been.

THE TINY CHURCH (11)

Turn off the A37 Dorchester/Yeovil road where signposted to Stockwood, almost opposite Melbury House. After a short distance the road bends sharply to the left then, on the right hand side, you will see a sign for Church Farm.

Please note that the driveway to the farm is in constant use by farm vehicles. It is best to park safely on the wide verge and walk the short distance from the road. The Church of St. Edwold is adjacent to the farmhouse and is reached through a gate on your left, thence over a small bridge which was once the only access. If the church is not open, the key is held in the farmhouse.

This is one of the smallest churches in England, being just 9 metres long and less than 4 metres wide. It is plain but very charming, with a circular bell turret on one gable. A guide book gives all the information and its modest cost helps The Churches Conservation Trust who now care for the building.

THE MILLER'S GRAVESTONE (12)

The Sydling Water once provided power for six mills between its source at Up Sydling and Grimstone, where it joins the River Frome. They all gradually fell into disuse and at the beginning of this century the last miller, Robert Spriggs, died. He was buried in Sydling churchyard and his headstone is one of the great mill stones of that era. It is a fitting memorial in a village where the Sydling Water still courses through, a reminder of industry in days gone by.

Miller's Gravestone, Sydling.

THE CROSS IN HAND (13)

Did four kings really cross hands at this high point and vow never to fight again? Was a murderer hanged in chains here? Or does this strange stone mark the spot where the holy bread was lost, then found again? Whichever legend you care to believe, the Cross in Hand is sited in a beautiful position 800 feet above sea level on Batcombe Down, between Holywell on the A37 and Minterne Magna on the A352.

Cross in Hand.

Some say the stone is merely a boundary marker; some, that pilgrims placed alms on the top. Certainly there is a nearby friary, tucked deep in a fold in the downs. Is it the base of a once taller statue with, perhaps, a cross on the top? Or did it once have a hand carved on one face, as reported in an early book on Dorset's stone crosses? Even its age is open to argument, from Roman to 14th century.

The favourite story is that of the lost pyx. A priest crossing Batcombe Down at night to administer the last rites to a dying man, unknowingly dropped the pyx containing the consecrated bread. Having discovered his loss he retraced his steps, searching without much hope of success. Suddenly he saw a pillar of fire come down from the sky, concentrating its light on one particular spot. When he reached that place, the pyx was restored to him.

Decide for yourself which legend you will believe by finding the stone at Gore Cross. It is just to the west of the cross-roads, on the right hand side heading west. Pick a clear day and you should be able to see both the English and Bristol Channels in the distance.

THE VICTORIAN POST BOX (14)

Holwell lies just south-east of Sherborne. Take the A3030 as far as Bishop's Caundle and turn right to Barnes Cross. Adjacent you will see a red letterbox outside a pair of cottages. This Victorian box was made by John N. Butt of Gloucester about 1855 and is believed to be the oldest still in use in Great Britain. The narrow vertical letter slot has an inner hinged flap to give protection which, coupled with the octagonal design, gives the box a quaint but decorative appearance.

There is another Victorian pillar box, in Dorchester at the junction of South Street and South Walks Road. It is not quite as old as the Holwell box, but still in use.

THE CERNE GIANT (15)

Of considerable height and age, this well-endowed chalk figure continues to mystify as he strides across the hillside above one of Dorset's prettiest villages. He could be Roman, perhaps Hercules. On the other hand, he could be a much more recent hoax. Locals are divided in their opinions.

The Giant wasn't mentioned in any of the Cerne Abbey documents, which is surprising, but if he represents a pagan belief, did they just ignore him? The Victorians allowed grass to cover his embarrassment - and theirs.

Victorian Pillar Box, Holywell.

You can walk up to the Giant by taking the path from the end of Abbey Street, but he was never meant to be seen at close quarters. The best view is from the lay-by just outside the village, to the north.

ST. AUGUSTINE'S WELL (16)

Abbey Street, Cerne Abbas, is bordered by a narrow stream which runs from a pretty pond at the northern end. The pond is filled by spring water from St. Augustine's Well, tucked into a deep hollow in the churchyard. Go through the metal gate and the Well is signed ahead and then down to your right.

The origin of the Well is lost in the mists of time, but it was possibly a pagan sacred site. If you look into the still waters at dawn on Easter Day, you may see the reflection of those who will die. Drinking the water is believed to cure infertility, perhaps linked with nocturnal activities on the Cerne Giant which are also said to produce results!

Spinsters prayed to St. Catherine for a husband at the Well and there is a small carving of a Catherine wheel on one of the stones. Any new born baby that eventually made its appearance could be dipped beneficially into the Well as the sun touched the water.

A useful little spring, particularly when the water spreads into the pond and down Abbey Street so charmingly.

LITERARY DORSET

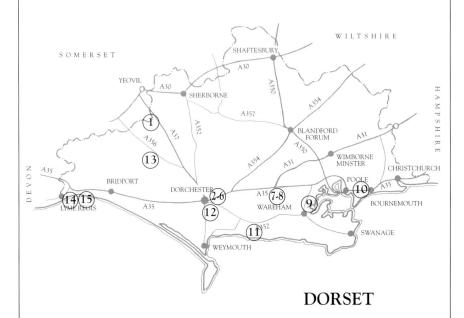

DORSET

THE THOMAS HARDY TOUR
1. Melbury Osmund
2. The cottage, Higher Bockhampton
3. The school, Lower Bockhampton
4. Max Gate
5. Stinsford churchyard
6. Eric Kennington's statue
   of Hardy, Dorchester

THE LAWRENCE OF ARABIA TOUR
7. Cloud's Hill
8. Moreton churchyard
9. Eric Kennington's effigy of Lawrence,
   Wareham

THE COUNTY CONNECTIONS TOUR
10. Robert Louis Stevenson
11. The Powys Brothers
12. William Barnes
13. Sylvia Townsend Warner
14. John Fowles
15. Jane Austen

LITERARY DORSET

Dorset's great sons of Thomas Hardy and William Barnes head a lengthy list of writers who have found inspiration in the county. The Powys brothers and Sylvia Townsend Warner also made their homes here, while John Fowles works still in Lyme Regis.

John Meade Falkner told a tale of Dorset smuggling in "Moonfleet", Henry Fielding used his surroundings at East Stour to give colour to "Tom Jones". Douglas Adams conceived "Hitch-hiker's Guide to the Galaxy" while visiting his parents in Stalbridge, while Bridport's bypass was reputedly the "Blott" that Tom Sharpe eventually put "on the Landscape".

Novelists and poets, their words live on. Perhaps none more so than those of Rupert Brooke, stationed at Blandford Army Camp at the beginning of this century: "If I should die, think only this of me: that there's some corner of a foreign field that is forever England".

The Thomas Hardy Tour

MELBURY OSMUND (1)

Driving from Dorchester to Yeovil along the A37, turn left just before the county boundary and follow the narrow road into Melbury Osmund. Here, a pretty cluster of thatched cottages curves round the church then down to a ford on the edge of the village.

It was in St. Osmund's church in 1839 that the hasty marriage took place between Jemima Hand and Thomas Hardy, stonemason. Their son, named Thomas after his father, was the boy who became Dorset's much-loved novelist and one of the great writers of the world.

HARDY'S COTTAGE, HIGHER BOCKHAMPTON (2)

The young Thomas was born on 2 June, 1840, in a cottage on the edge of the great heath. It was the Hardy family home, built by Thomas's great-grandfather for his grandparents, and the first five of Hardy's novels were penned there.

Higher Bockhampton is just to the east of Dorchester. There is a car park at the edge of the forest but the cottage is about another half mile on foot. There are many waymarked paths and nature trails, with picnic tables for those who wish to make a day of it. The woods are especially beautiful at bluebell time, carpets of the flowers laying a deep blue haze as far as the eye can see.

The Hardy family lived in the cottage until 1912. In 1948 it became the property of the National Trust and is now open to the public. An appointment must be made with the custodian to view the interior (01305-262366). The cottage is usually open daily except Fridays and Saturdays, from April to October. Adjacent to the cottage is a memorial to Thomas Hardy erected by the Americans who enjoy his descriptive Wessex novels.

THE SCHOOL, LOWER BOCKHAMPTON (3)

A short distance away as the crow flies is Lower Bockhampton, picturesque with its old cottages and bridges over the River Frome. It lies on the edge of the Kingston Maurward estate, now an agricultural college, which has many fine and mature trees as well as lovely gardens which are open to the public. Kingston Maurward was the setting for Hardy's second novel - the first to be accepted for publication, in 1871 - called "Desperate Remedies".

The small school in the village was where Thomas studied his three Rs. Did he show promise then of his fine mind? He trained as an architect with John Hicks in Dorchester before moving to a London practice, then returned to the county town in 1867 and began to write the stories which were to bring Wessex to the world.

MAX GATE, DORCHESTER (4)

In 1874, "Far from the Madding Crowd" provided enough money for Hardy to marry his sweetheart, Emma Gifford. Over the next ten years he found fame and financial stability. The couple settled in Dorchester, renting a cottage in Glyde Path Road (Shire Hall Lane as it was then called) before moving into a house that Hardy himself had designed on the edge of town.

Max Gate, named after the old toll house known as Mack's Gate, was to be Hardy's home until he died in 1928. It was very close to Came Rectory, where William Barnes lived and wrote his poetry in Dorset dialect, and the two were good friends. Hardy's study from Max Gate can be seen in the Dorset County Museum in Dorchester.

Max Gate is owned by the National Trust and part is open only by appointment with the tenants (01305-262538) from April to September; Mondays, Wednesdays and Sundays; p.m. only.

STINSFORD CHURCHYARD (5)

Hardy survived his first wife Emma and, aged 74, married his secretary Florence Dugdale who was half his age. When he died in 1928, aged 87, it was thought fitting that his ashes should be taken to Poet's Corner in Westminster Abbey. His heart was buried in Emma's grave in Stinsford churchyard, almost mid-way between the house where he died and the cottage where he was born.

Hardy was a frequent visitor to St. Michael's church where he, his father and grandfather all played in the church band. The musician's gallery was later removed, but has recently been reinstated and inaugurated with the playing of some of the old instruments with which Hardy would have been very familiar.

Thomas Hardy's statue, Dorchester.

HARDY'S STATUE, DORCHESTER (6)

The life and works of Thomas Hardy are commemorated in the fine bronze statue at Top o' Town, Dorchester. It was sculpted by Eric Kennington and unveiled in 1931. Hardy sits gazing peacefully ahead, perhaps how he would have looked while pondering on the story line for his next novel.

The statue is never without visitors. On Hardy anniversaries it is quite common for wreaths to be laid at the foot of the plinth. On New Year's Eve, occasionally the old man sports a nifty hat. He takes it all in his stride.

The Lawrence of Arabia Tour

CLOUD'S HILL (7)

T E Lawrence was born in 1888 in Tremadog, North Wales. He began the First World War as an Intelligence Officer in the Arab Bureau in Egypt and became totally involved in the volatile political situation.

Following his Arabian exploits which earned him much acclaim he sought isolation and anonymity, joining the Tank Corps in 1923 under a pseudonym. He was posted to Bovington Army Camp and its tank training grounds, but soon found a small cottage nearby, Cloud's Hill, first renting and eventually buying.

Lawrence's lifestyle seemed most strange to his friends who visited him there. Books everywhere, a panelled music room, but no kitchen where even the most basic of meals could be prepared. "Why worry?" inscribed in Greek over the door must have seemed very appropriate.

Lawrence's book "Seven Pillars of Wisdom" was polished and finally sent to the publishers from here.

MORETON CHURCHYARD (8)

Always a motorbike fanatic, Lawrence was involved in an accident with two cyclists while riding not far from Cloud's Hill on 13 May 1935. His death occurred in hospital six days later. An enigmatic character in life, his death caused even more questions to be asked about the man and his role.

There was a feeling among some that Lawrence, far from being out on a limb in the wilds of Dorset, was being trained to head a secret service type organisation. Others were sure his death was no accident and there was talk of a mysterious car that had been involved. Many notable people attended his funeral at Moreton, including Sir Winston Churchill, who shed tears as he commented that we should never see the like of Lawrence again.

Lawrence was buried in Moreton churchyard where, each year on the anniversary of his death, a bouquet of roses mysteriously appears; one bloom less each year.

St. Martin's Church, Wareham, which contains Eric Kennington's fine effigy of Lawrence of Arabia.

LAWRENCE'S MAGNIFICENT STATUE, WAREHAM (9)

Eric Kennington, who sculpted the statue of Hardy in Dorchester, was commissioned to produce a memorial to Lawrence. This he did, showing the man in full Arab clothing resting with his head on a camel saddle. It was intended that this great work should be placed in Salisbury Cathedral.

Lawrence had been a most controversial figure, notably because of the whispers of homosexuality which surrounded him and, as the time approached for the effigy to be put in position, the Dean of Salisbury regretfully declined the offer.

Eventually the Saxon Church of St. Martin in Wareham offered a resting place and it is here that the striking sculpture can be seen today.

The County Connections Tour

ROBERT LOUIS STEVENSON and "Kidnapped" (10)

Bournemouth, because of its mild climate, attracted many who were in need of convalescence. One such was Robert Louis Stevenson who arrived in 1884, also taking the opportunity of being closer to his stepson who was at school nearby and who later collaborated in some of Stevenson's work.

R. L. Stevenson plaque, Westbourne.

The author set up home at no: 61 Alum Chine Road. He called the house "Skerryvore", after the lighthouse on the Argyle coast of Scotland which had been built by his family. It was destroyed by bombs at the end of 1940, but the site has been preserved as a memorial garden to the author.

While at Skerryvore, Stevenson wrote "Kidnapped" and "The Strange Case of Dr. Jekyll and Mr. Hyde". His other adventure stories of "Treasure Island" and "The Black Arrow" are classics, while "Travels with a Donkey in the Cevennes" remains a favourite.

The memorial plaque to the author can be found on one of the bridges crossed on the pleasant walk down Alum Chine.

THE POWYS BROTHERS (11)

Theodore F Powys, born in 1875, moved to East Chaldon in Dorset aged twenty-nine and lived there for the next thirty-five years. He was a prolific writer with titles such as "The Left Leg", "The Two Thieves" and, set in his own village, "Mr. Weston's Good Wine".

He was one of three literary brothers. Llewelyn lived nearby for fourteen years and John Cowper was also there for short periods. They attracted others with similar talents, notably the writer Sylvia Townsend Warner and sculptress Elizabeth Muntz.

Muntz sculpted the head of T. F. Powys, which is now in the Dorset County museum, and also inscribed a memorial stone to Llewelyn. It can be found near the coast, one mile north-east of White Nothe. Follow the path up from East Chaldon past Chideock Farm and then turn west towards the 178m trig point.

WILLIAM BARNES, Dorset's dialect poet (12)

No single attribution can be made to Barnes, born on Bagber Common near Sturminster Newton in 1801. This astonishing man, who left school at the age of thirteen, was first a school-master in Mere and Dorchester then, following the successful completion of a ten year part-time degree in divinity, became rector of both Came and Whitcombe just outside the county town.

He was familiar with sixty-five languages, wrote knowledgeably on many subjects including archaeology, was musician, artist and playwright. His friends included the poets Tennyson and Browning and, closer to home, the novelist Thomas Hardy.

Barnes is best known for his poems written in the Dorset dialect, which have been "translated" into plain English for those who wish to read them more easily. To hear them in the original dialect, as they are presented sometimes at special events, is to gain added pleasure from the soft Dorset inflections and the simple, often humorous, scenes he depicted so well.

Barnes died while at Came Rectory, a pretty cottage on the Wareham road not far from Dorchester. His imposing statue, in knee breeches and frock coat, stands outside St. Peter's Church in the county town. He is buried in the churchyard at Winterborne Came.

SYLVIA TOWNSEND WARNER (13)

Riverside Cottage in Frome Lane, Frome Vauchurch, on the edge of Maiden

Newton, was home to the poet and writer Sylvia Townsend Warner for forty years. Born in 1893, the daughter of a Harrow schoolmaster, this most gifted of writers used her many talents and enthusiasms to interest and enchant readers until her death in 1978.

Books such as "Lolly Willowes" flowed from her pen, with a pause only while she followed her conscience and went to take part in the Spanish Civil War with Valentine Cunningham, her lifelong companion.

She was attracted to Dorset and, firstly, East Chaldon (Chaldon Herring) by the Powys brothers who had made the tiny village their home. She then bought a house at Frome Vauchurch, near Maiden Newton, where she lived for forty years.

In death she returned to East Chaldon and is buried in the churchyard there.

JOHN FOWLES and "The French Lieutenant's Woman" (14)

If you know Lyme Regis, you know the Cobb. If you know the Cobb, chances are you already have a mental picture of that dark-cloaked heroine forlornly watching the stormy sea - "The French Lieutenant's Woman".

John Fowles wrote the novel in 1969 while living in Pound Street. Set in Napoleonic times, the story takes place in and around Lyme Regis. It is atmospheric and beautifully descriptive of this small seaside town and its beaches, made famous by the wealth of fossils to be found, if you are lucky.

JANE AUSTEN and "Persuasion" (15)

Lyme Regis was also used by Jane Austen as the setting for part of "Persuasion". The authoress was a frequent visitor to the town at the beginning of the 19th century and also uses the Cobb to good effect in her story-telling.

No-one is quite sure where she stayed, but Austen is commemorated by the Jane Austen Garden, between the Cobb and Marine Parade.

THREE RIVERS AND THEIR VALLEYS

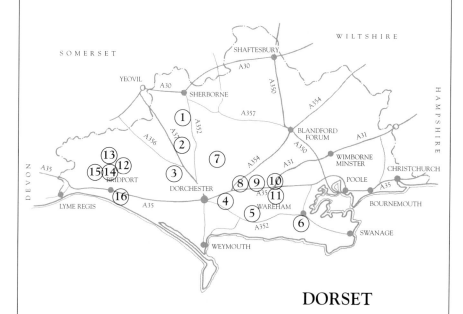

DORSET

THE FROME TOUR
1. The source, Evershot
2. Cattistock
3. Wren's Bridge, Frampton
4. Woodsford Castle
5. The engraved windows, Moreton
6. Wareham Quay

THE PIDDLE TOUR
7. Piddletrenthide school gates
8. Musician's gallery, Puddletown church
9. Athelhampton House
10. The Martyr's Tree, Tolpuddle
11. Briantspuddle and Culpepper's Dish

THE BRIT TOUR
12. Hooke Park
13. Beaminster
14. Netherbury
15. Pilsdon Pen
16. Bridport

THREE RIVERS AND THEIR VALLEYS

Dorset has two major rivers, the Frome and the Stour, plus many smaller watercourses which include two 'winterbornes'.

The one that every child loves is the River Piddle with its associated rude-sounding place names, so it is for their delight I have included it in this section. It rises just north of Alton Pancras towards the centre of the county and finds its way through valleys and heaths to Poole Harbour.

The River Frome rises to the west, in the chalk downs at Evershot, gathering its five main tributaries of the Hooke, Sydling Water, Cerne, South Winterborne and Tadnoll Brook before it, too, flows into Poole Harbour close to the Piddle. Only Wareham keeps them apart.

The River Brit is small by comparison, rising near Beaminster and the hillforts of Pilsdon and Lewesdon. It is fed by the Mangerton, which rises in Hooke Park. They jointly reach the sea at West Bay.

The river valleys are full of interest: villages, bridges and churches set among a landscape that can offer peace and seclusion even in the middle of the tourist season.

The River Frome Tour

THE SOURCE, AT EVERSHOT (1)

To first see the light of day between Girt Lane and Dirty Lane, in a place firmly on record as being of "noe note" (Coker's Survey of Dorsetshire), is the inauspicious beginning of the River Frome. It rises at St. John's Well; a quiet seeping of water from the chalk as Dorset's second largest river gathers initial momentum on its long journey to Poole Harbour.

Evershot, one of the highest villages in the county, is nevertheless tucked deep in a green valley to the west of the A37, the Dorchester/Yeovil highway. Part of the A35 is still known as Long Ash Lane and was the Roman road between Dorchester and Ilchester.

The Church of St. Osmund sports an exuberant corner pinnacle and clock. Inside, a rare brass of a chaliced priest, William Grey, rector of Evershot from 1511 until his death in 1524. A later rector, George Crabbe, wrote the story of "Peter Grimes" which was set to music by Benjamin Britten in 1945.

The source of the River Frome is just inside Back Lane, behind the church. Close by is Tess Cottage, where in Thomas Hardy's novel "Tess of the d'Urbervilles" his heroine stopped to take refreshment.

At the lower end of the village are the lion-topped piers guarding the entrance into Melbury deer park. There is a lovely walk through the park to Melbury Osmund giving glimpses of great Melbury House where, occasionally, the gardens are open to the public.

CATTISTOCK (2)

Famous for its Hunt, Cattistock is one of the largest Dorset villages. The Church of St. Peter & St. Paul has a slender and beautiful tower which once boasted a carillon of thirty-five bells. Silenced at the outbreak of war in 1939, almost exactly one year later they were destroyed by a fire in the tower, melted by the intense heat. The tower was left in such a dangerous condition that it was dismantled, every stone being numbered before being laid out in a nearby field. It was rebuilt at the end of the war.

Cattistock.

The Hunt started in the mid-18th century as the "True Blue". Its popularity was such that the White Horse Inn which served the village soon became "The Fox & Hounds". The village has strong connections with the Royal Navy and has given its name to three Hunt Class ships this century.

The nearby earthwork, Castle Hill, extends to about four acres. There are two ramped causeway entrances through its earth banks. The purpose of the site is unclear, but it would have been easily defensible high ground in a skirmish between tribes.

WREN'S BRIDGE, FRAMPTON (3)

There are some nasty bends on the road through this mainly linear village and it pays to remain alert at the wheel. However if you park the car somewhere safe and explore on foot, there is a lot to be seen. There used to be two villages here,

Wren's Bridge, Frampton.

Southover and Northover, now linked in the parish name of Frampton. Southover still remains, a tiny detached group of farms and cottages to the south of the River Frome.

The Church of St. Mary the Virgin was unwittingly the cause of the one-sided nature of the village today. In 1796, lead repairs being carried out on the roof caused sparks to fly across the road onto a row of thatched cottages. Forty-three were destroyed in the blaze and were never rebuilt, the adjacent parkland being extended and enclosed in the wall that still stands.

Opposite the church there is a gate in the wall, no longer used. The residents of the great house, Frampton Court, used to walk this way to church across a small, white bridge. Squire Algernon Browne of the Court was buried near here, close to the river that he loved. The vicar, with whom he was said to be often at odds, was heard to remark that "the dear departed would probably end up in Poole Harbour". By the mid-19th century the house had become the property of the Sheridans, descendants of Richard Brinsley Sheridan, poet and dramatist.

The six bells of St. Mary's are rung with an eye on the splendid exhortation of 1814: "By Rule and Order of the Belfry, There's neither Music, Voice or Song Can be compar'd to Bells well rung. Take off your hat, Coat and Spurs."

Walk across the River Frome towards Southover and take the lane on your left that leads past Frampton Court, towards Muckleford. A few hundred yards walking through parkland landscaped by Lancelot 'Capability' Brown brings you to Frampton Park Bridge, known locally as Wren's Bridge. Built in Portland stone to a design reputedly by Sir Christopher Wren, this is a curvaceous and beautifully proportioned bridge.

Squire Browne, on being advised that the river was too narrow to accommodate the planned three-arch bridge apparently replied: "Then widen it!" So they did, and the result, admired by many, was worth the effort.

THE THATCHED CASTLE, WOODSFORD (4)

A fortified manor house, this early 14th century builing is now owned by the Landmark Trust and is enjoyed as a holiday let - if you don't mind the resident ghost. Built of Purbeck limestone, its thatched roof (one of the largest in the country) replaces the crenellations that had been added during the turbulent Middle Ages. Many wealthy landowners then found it prudent to ensure their families and possessions had more security.

Royal permission had to be sought before manor houses such as Woodsford and Herringston on the River Frome, and nearby Athelhampton on the River Piddle, could be fortified as domestic strongholds.

THE ENGRAVED WINDOWS, MORETON (5)

Moreton boasts the longest footbridge in Dorset, the grave of the legendary Lawrence of Arabia, and beautiful church windows.

The Church of St. Nicholas was substantially damaged by a bomb dropped by enemy aircraft at the end of 1940. It took ten years to rebuild, with war damage money paying for the first of five new windows engraved on plain glass by Laurence Whistler. These windows with subsequent additions fill the church with a wonderful quality of light which greatly enhances the interior.

The windows in the semi-circular apse, the first to receive engraved glass, depict the bombed shell of the church and the building newly restored. Other subjects are the seasons, fruitfulness, light and darkness, plus a window of lightning in which the jagged forks chart the courses of the Rivers Piddle and Frome nearby.

The church now has twelve Whistler windows, the offer of a thirteenth in 1994 sadly resulting in controversy. It shows the suicide of Judas Iscariot, the thirty pieces of silver turning to flowers as they drop from his hand to the earth. Parishioners decided that the theme of suicide and guilt was inappropriate and the window is now on permanent loan to the Dorset County Museum in High West Street, Dorchester. Laurence Whistler has offered it to Moreton as a gift, with no time limit on acceptance, so one day it may yet find itself beside the River Frome.

THE QUAY, WAREHAM (6)

Where better to end a day out than at Wareham, sandwiched between the Rivers Frome and Piddle as they finally reach Poole Harbour. The gateway to Purbeck, the town was a fortified Saxon 'burh' with town walls which are believed to date from King Alfred's reign.

Wareham Quay, where the River Frome nears its end at Poole Harbour.

At the time of the Norman Conquest, Wareham and Bridport were listed as the county's two main ports. The town's position at the head of the harbour provided a sheltered anchorage, with protection from land attack afforded by nearby Corfe Castle.

Gradually the size of ships increased, sail taking over from oar, and Wareham's disadvantages began to weigh heavily. Manoeuvring in the Wareham Channel, trying to make headway under sail against blustery south-westerlies, became increasingly difficult in limited waters. The gradual silting up at the mouth of the Frome probably added to the port's decline. Local sea-farers began to consider establishing themselves nearer the harbour mouth at Poole, where the benefits of being closer to the main shipping route were obvious. By the mid-14th century Wareham had been ousted as a major port.

The quay is still busy with small yachts and other vessels, while local inns and restaurants provide the perfect end to a journey down the Frome.

The River Piddle Tour

PIDDLETRENTHIDE SCHOOL GATES (7)

The school in the centre of the village has unusual iron gates, with spear-headed uprights and cable moulding. They once surrounded a royal tomb in Westminster Abbey.

In the early 19th century railings were removed from several of the Abbey tombs. Three sets were sold to John Bridge of Piddletrenthide Manor, who was a jeweller and silversmith on Ludgate Hill. Mr Bridge was well known for collecting unusual items and the railings were brought back to his home in the Piddle valley.

Mr Bridge's railings came from the tombs of Mary, Queen of Scots; Lady Margaret Beaufort, mother of King Henry VII; Margaret, Countess of Lennox.

Mr Bridge died in 1834 and when, in 1848, the village school was built, his daughters presented one set of railings to be used as gates. No-one was certain from which of the tombs the 'gates' had come, but the thought that they could have surrounded Mary, Queen of Scots, caused much comment.

However when the rest of the collection was auctioned in 1911, provenance was found for the two remaining sets of railings. If the auctioneers did their homework correctly, the gates at Piddletrenthide School came from the tomb of Margaret, Countess of Lennox. Her son Lord Darnley had at one time been married to Mary, Queen of Scots so the tenuous royal connection is still there.

MUSICIAN'S GALLERY, PUDDLETOWN CHURCH (8)

Village bands were a traditional part of Dorset life. Fiddle, flute and clarinet were popular instruments played for many events but, most particularly, the band led the congregation in church, often from an ornate gallery especially for their use.

One such gallery is in the church at Puddletown, where the date of 1635 is carved into the timber. Occasionally some of the old instruments are on display. The carvings in the church where much of the woodwork is 17th century is particularly fine, with the pulpit and box pews worth more than a glance.

ATHELHAMPTON HOUSE (9)

Following a serious fire, this beautiful Tudor house has emerged, like a phoenix, from the ashes. The interior is splendid and was used to film Michael Caine and Laurence Olivier in "Sleuth".

The gardens are beautiful, bounded and divided by decorative stone walls and balustrading. The yew pyramids on the clipped grass contrast wonderfully with the wilder walk that edges the River Piddle. There are ponds, statues, colourful borders, and a dovecote on the lead roof of which Thomas Hardy scratched his name.

Search for the chained ape of the family motto: "He who looks at Martyn's ape, Martyn's ape shall look at him".

There is a small tea room at Athelhampton and a visit can be extended over several hours if the weather is fine.

THE MARTYRS' TREE, TOLPUDDLE (10)

Six farm labourers from Tolpuddle were sentenced to transportation in 1834, as a result of making a loyal pledge and forming an agricultural union to better their prospects. There was nothing illegal in the union, but angry and worried landowners ensured the men were successfully accused of "administering an unlawful oath" under an Act passed in 1797 to quell a naval mutiny and never repealed.

They were tried in the Old Crown Court in Dorchester and the Tolpuddle Martyrs, as they became known, roused the country to outcry at the severity of their sentence. The six were pardoned three years later but only one, James Hammett, returned to England and Tolpuddle. When he died he was buried in the churchyard there. The rest settled in Canada.

The men used to meet under a massive sycamore tree on the village green, the Martyrs' Tree. Only the stump remains, a new tree planted nearby to take its place. There is an interesting museum to the west of the village which gives a history of Trade Union movement. The six cottages were built as a memorial to the Martyrs by the TUC in 1934.

BRIANTSPUDDLE AND CULPEPPER'S DISH (11)

A "model village" built by Sir Ernest Debenham, a London draper, between 1919 and 1932 lies in the quiet Bladon Valley. It was an attempt at self-sufficiency, the estate including a dairy, chicken farm, bee-keeping, forestry and livestock. The unusual thatched 20th century houses in the Arts & Crafts style blend in with older cottages and there is a fine war memorial by Eric Gill.

Half a mile south is an enormous swallow hole called Culpepper's Dish. It is about 280' in diameter and 70' deep. These holes are believed to have been caused by water scouring away the chalk. There are fully grown trees in the bottom which reach to the rim. The area is a favourite picnic spot.

The Brit Tour

HOOKE PARK (12)

Close to Beaminster, springs form the source of the River Brit between the hillforts of Pilsdon Pen and Lewesdon. At Hooke Park between Mapperton and Toller the Mangerton River begins, which joins the Brit just before the sea.

There are 340 acres of mixed woodland criss-crossed by bridleways and public footpaths. The wildlife is varied and you may be lucky enough to see badger or deer. There are birds of many species, from bluetits to hawks; butterflies; and a wealth of flowers. Hooke Park at bluebell time is a sight to be remembered.

The park is owned and managed by the Parnham Trust. It is also the site of an interesting experiment in ecologically designed timber houses, some of which can be viewed by the public. Entrance to this area is off the B3163 east of Beaminster. It is open one or two days a week from Easter to October, and usually on Bank Holidays. There is a small charge but children under 10 are free. Further information from 01308-863130.

BEAMINSTER (13)

If you're a brandy drinker, then the name of Thomas Hine will be familiar. Cognac Hine takes its name from a son of Beaminster. Thomas was born in 1775 and, at 17 years of age, left to find fortune in France. He took employment in Jarnac on the River Charente, centre of the cognac industry.

Not only did Thomas learn the business thoroughly, he also fell in love with his boss's daughter. In time he became a partner in the business, then the owner. He died when anly 47 years old, in 1822, but by then had given his name to the king of cognacs.

This pretty, bustling little town has seen many local industries come and go, including rope, sail cloth and paper making, but is especially known for the clockmakers who have spread its name more widely.

NETHERBURY (14)

Still on the subject of drinking but perhaps rather more 'downmarket', the pretty village of Netherbury was the centre of good cider making in the mid-18th century. The power of the River Brit was once harnessed here for corn and flax mills.

Take a look inside the church at the brasses of the Hood family, famous seafarers, and find your way up to the W. Rhodes Moorhouse memorial on a nearby hill, commemorating the first airman to be awarded the Victoria Cross.

PILSDON PEN (15)

No visit to the area would be complete without a climb up Pilsdon Pen, one of Dorset's Iron Age hillforts. Together with neighbouring Lewesdon, the pair nicknamed "Cow and Calf", sailors have used the hills as navigation markers for centuries.

Views over the surrounding countryside make the effort well worthwhile and provide a superb picnic spot. There is a National Trust car park.

BRIDPORT (16)

Where the Brit nears the sea, Bridport stands, its history firmly in the rope and net making that is still carried on here after many centuries. The industry began with ropes for ships' rigging, expanded into net making for the fishermen, and has included such diverse items as tennis nets and rope for the hangman's noose (such death being referred to as "being stabbed with a Bridport dagger"!).

The town should be explored on foot, with its narrow back streets - the 'rope walks' - and fine buildings such' as the Town Hall. Take a stroll to the bottom of South Street and West Bay Road to see Palmer's Brewery, still with its thatched roof and water wheel. There is an excellent museum and plenty of antique shops, plus a Saturday market which fills the main street with colour.

COAST AND COUNTRY

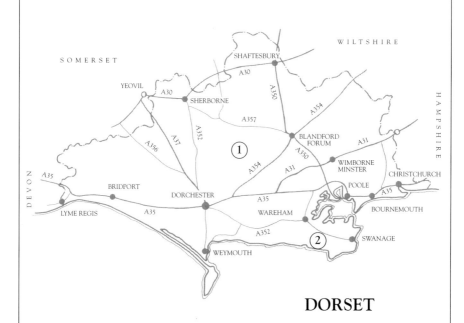

DORSET

1. THE DORSET GAP WALK

2. THE TYNEHAM CAP WALK

WALK 1 - THE DORSET GAP

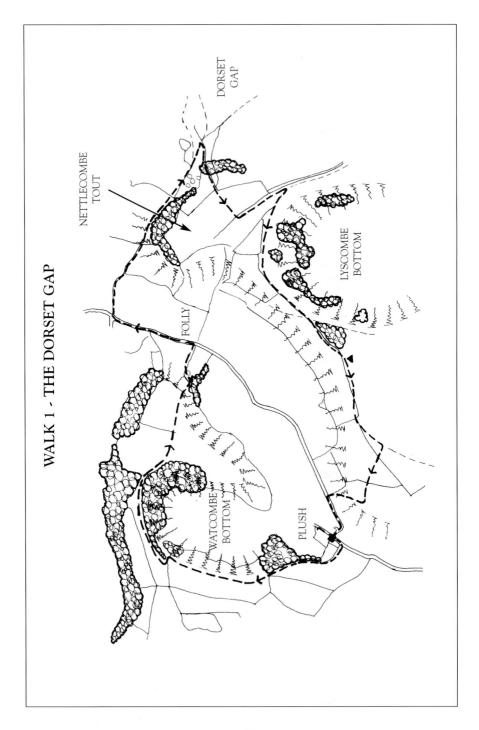

DORSET GAP

NETTLECOMBE TOUT

LYSCOMBE BOTTOM

FOLLY

WATCOMBE BOTTOM

PLUSH

WALK COAST AND COUNTRY

I make no apology for including in this book two walks which will stretch your muscles and your stamina. We have become a four-wheeled nation, often steering clear of any excursion that involves leaving the car behind. Of course there are those for whom transport is a necessity and happily there are many lovely places in Dorset close to a convenient lay-by or car park.

Those that are young in heart and sound in wind and limb: no excuses! There is no better way to see this beautiful county, enjoy the landscape and hear the silence. Best foot forward as you follow these two routes. Sensible shoes are recommended but, provided the weather is fine, you should encounter no more than a little rough going here and there.

CENTRE COUNTY AND THE DORSET GAP (1)

A distance of 7 miles or so, this takes about 2.5 hours walking. There are one or two steady hill climbs but plenty of level striding, too The three main attractions are far reaching views in all directions, the chance to add your name and comments to those already encased in the biscuit box of notebooks at the Dorset Gap, and last, but not least, the "Brace of Pheasants" at Plush where you start and finish.

The walk is marked in many places by Dorset County Council direction discs and by the gryphon logo of the Wessex Ridgeway. If you want to be doubly assured, take the Pathfinder 1299 map in your pocket.

Park in the tiny village of Plush, east of Piddletrenthide. Walk down through the village past the pub and turn right after "Little Platt", signed to Alton Pancras. This is a steady pull uphill, through one wide gate. Keep going until you reach the second where, just inside, is a clear and helpful County Council map of the terrain. Ahead is a wide open pasture, while to your right the ground drops steeply away into the bowl of Watcombe Bottom. Follow the lip of the Bottom which leads ahead and then to the right, aiming for the top right hand corner of the pasture. You will pass a large, concrete water trough en route.

Through the gate, the narrowed pasture extends ahead with a large hedgerow both to left and right. Turn left and follow the short track which takes you to the far side of the left hand hedge, then turn right, keeping the hedge on your right.

Following the line of the hedge, you will soon come to an area about the size of a medium house plot, in a raised bank. This ancient enclosure is just one of the many earthworks that pepper the county, a sign of occupation perhaps three thousand years ago. The field ends with another gateway, the first of many with the Wessex Ridgeway marker disc. Go straight through, keeping to the edge of Watcombe Wood; over a stile, along the edge of a fields and then through a gate into a narrow path which descends steeply between banks to Folly.

Turn left at the road through Folly and walk along it until a right turn is signed to Spring Wood Farm, about half a mile. Head up the farm drive. A large metal gate on your right almost opposite the house, then another on your left in just a few yards, enable you to skirt the barns clear of the farmyard and make for the gate in the left hand corner of the field, under the tree-topped bulk of Nettlecombe Tout, one of Dorset's Iron Age hillforts.

Keeping the Tout on your right hand side, walk the path ahead until you reach a fence and follow its line uphill to your right. At the top, stop to look back over the Blackmore Vale; a stunning view which, on a clear day, stretches for mile after mile. Pass through two gates close together on the ridge and then walk the edge of the field downhill to two more gates, both with marker discs. Take the right hand path through the trees - it can be a bit nettley, so watch out for bare legs - and suddenly you emerge into sunshine and see the faded, green box marked "Dorset Gap".

The 'letter box' at the Dorset Gap.

When you have read the books and added your own comments, there is a good lunch stop just ahead on a high ridge overlooking Melcombe Park. The wild flowers are remarkable, even quite late in the year.

Leave the Gap, following the signpost marked Folly. The path soon veers left, leading into a field then heading for the top right hand corner. The gate here leads into a much larger field where, ahead and just to the left, there is a water tower which is your next marker. Turn left at the tower, keeping the hedgerow on your left, and walk to the next gate and through it.

Turn right along the fence then, after 100 metres, turn right through a small pedestrian gate. Dropping steeply away on your left is a beautiful dish of land called Lyscombe Bottom. Follow the path as it winds round the edge of the Bottom, through three small gates. If you look south you can see the glint of the sea at Poole Harbour. To the west, Hardy's Monument stands above Portesham.

Almost at the far side of the Bottom a larger gate leads into an area of pasture by a copse. After about 70 metres go through a gate an your right but keep walking in the same direction, along the edge of the trees. Once clear of the trees keep following the fence line, past the pyramidal 'trig' point in the adjoining field. Below, to your right, you can see Plush. Just a few more directions and you're home.

The next gate in the corner of the field leads through to the left hand side of the fence, but then keep walking in the same direction. After about another 250 metres you reach a gate on your right. Pass through, heading towards Plush in the valley. The path leads across two stiles before zig-zagging down into the village. Turn left and follow the lane back to the "Brace of Pheasants" - and a long, cool drink.

TYNEHAM CAP, KIMMERIDGE BAY AND WORBARROW TOUT (2)

The demands of 20th century warfare have resulted in the most beautiful section of the Dorset Coast Path falling within Army firing ranges. A spectacular walk past Tyneham, Kimmeridge and Worbarrow Tout provides scenery that is second to none while, just to the north of the Purbeck Hills, tank tracks have turned Povington Heath into a lunar landscape.

Despite being inaccessible for much of the time the Lulworth Range Walks are open regularly, usually at week-ends, public and school holidays. The narrow roads serving the area are all well signposted and give advance warning as to whether there is current access to MoD land. Range Walks are well marked, their yellow-topped posts clear in even the murkiest of weather. The golden rule is, stick to them.

The approach by car from any direction climbs to the spine of the Purbeck Hills between West Creech Hill and Whiteway Hill, with far-reaching views of Poole Harbour to the east and inland towards Cranborne Chase. The Povington car park provides a safe stopping point to enjoy magnificent views south and west.

Tyneham is tucked deep in the valley below. There is a steep walk down from here but, if you can't face the return haul at the end of a hot day, is better to drive into the village itself and use the extensive car parks there.

Leave the car park and walk south through a wide gate. The lane leads off to the right and Worbarrow Bay, but immediately ahead is a stile and zig-zag track scaling the flank of Gad Cliff. Once on the coastal ridge, turn east towards Tyneham Cap where, for an early breather, you will find a substantial stone seat tucked in under a sheltering wall.

The downhill path from here skirts Brandy Bay and Hobarrow Bay to Broad Bench, but that is the return journey. Keep walking east on the high ground until you reach the red warning flag - or its pole - at the corner of the MoD land. Turn south and down, watching the marker posts carefully. There is one obvious (unmarked) track; the correct path is not so easy to spot.

The path drops down the hill and eventually passes Dorset's inshore oil well and the "nodding donkey" pump. You reach the sea at the edge of Kimmeridge Bay with the Clavel Tower, an early 19th century folly, on the opposite headland. There are several seats and picnic tables; an ideal spot for lunch.

Kimmeridge is a great beach for doing things. When the tide is out, the ledges are exposed; slabs of shale lying horizontally, but staggered, like a mass of toppled dominoes. Rock pools make exploration a must, with the possibility of finding a fossil nearer the cliffs. An underwater wildlife reserve attracts divers throughout the summer. There is pedestrian access at the west end and a car park to the east if you drive through Kimmeridge on the toll road.

The Coast Path now runs west to Broad Bench, wide and grassy underfoot. Black and white oyster-catchers are distinctive visitors, with their long orange beaks. Turn

WALK 2 - THE TYNEHAM CAP

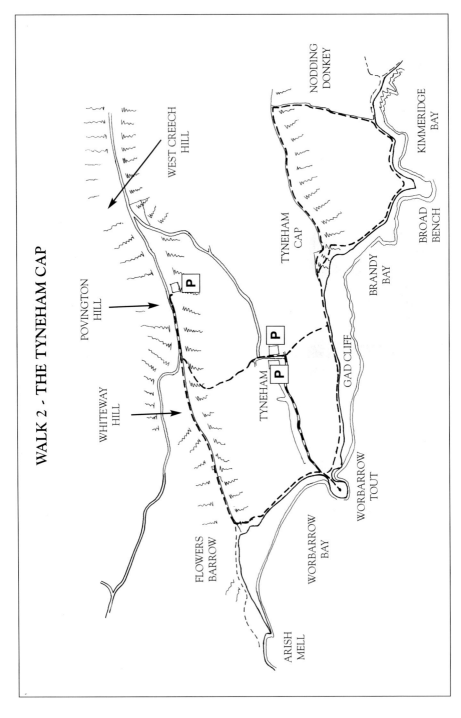

uphill with a bit more effort to the stone seat at Tyneham Cap again. Coastal erosion is a continuing problem and signs warning of minor diversions are to be expected.

View to Arish Mell, across Worbarrow bay.

The marked path is retraced along Gad Cliff, continuing past the descent to Tyneham until you scramble down a deeply rutted and stony track to Worbarrow Tout.

The sweep of Worbarrow Bay and the narrow entrance into Arish Mell form the view, with the Iron Age hillfort called Flowers Barrow on the ridge overlooking the sea.

The conical Tout must be climbed. It is an unusual formation of gypsum and Purbeck marble, joined to the mainland by the narrowest of necks. A quick burst of energy will get you to the top and a sheltered depression where you may sit in shirt sleeves mid-winter while basking in the trapped warmth of a pale sun.

If you left your car above Tyneham in the Povington car park, there is an alternative return route by following a steep path up the edge of Worbarrow Bay to Flowers Barrow and then turning east. The climb is very slippery underfoot in all but the driest weather.

The stony lane from Worbarrow Tout gives an easier last few hundred metres back to Tyneham's car park. You will have walked about 5 miles. If you have time, spend your last half-hour in deserted Tyneham. Drive back to the top of the ridge and look down just once again before going home, totally satisfied.

The OS Outdoor Leisure Map of Purbeck 1:25,000 scale covers the walk and surrounding area.

ANTIQUES AND CRAFTS

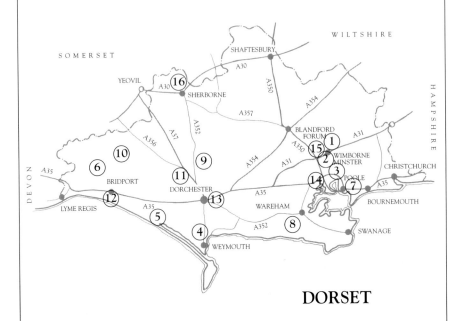

DORSET

THE CRAFTS TOUR
1. Walford Mill
2. Stapehill Abbey
3. Courtyard Centre
4. Brewers Quay
5. Dansel Gallery
6. Broadwindsor

THE POTTERY TOUR
7. Poole Pottery
8. Blue Pool
9. Abbey Pottery
10. Shepherd's Well Pottery
11. New Barn Field Centre

THE ANTIQUES TOUR
12. Bridport Antiques Centre
13. De Danaan Centre
14. Old Button Shop Antiques
15. Wimborne Antiques Bazaar
16. Antiques Nook

ANTIQUES AND CRAFTS

Antiques and crafts: both words seem to have become over-used and undervalued, meaning anything from a local turn-out at a car boot sale to imported foreign goods which bear no relation at all to the place in which they are being sold.

In this section I have tried to search out some of the best places to find both. I have not included specialist antique shops, assuming that on holiday you are more likely to be looking for a bargain or a good selection through which to trawl. Crafts tend to be in centres, where two or more are gathered together in the pursuit of excellence. Quality is everywhere, but you may still be surprised at the affordable price tags.

Pottery has been given a tour of its own. As long ago as the Romans, pottery and salt played an important part in the economy of Poole Harbour. This pottery, 'exported' by ship to Hadrian's Wall on the Scottish border, was long-lasting and very popular with the garrisons stationed there. It is known as black burnished ware. Poole pottery is still as collectable now, as it was then.

The Crafts Tour

WALFORD MILL CRAFT CENTRE (1)

Hat making at Walford Mill, Wimborne.

Opened by the Dorset Craft Guild in 1986, Walford Mill Craft Centre has gone from strength to strength. Exciting exhibitions as well as eye-catching displays of the very best in British craft and design make it a "must" if you are looking for a special gift.

There has been a mill on this site for centuries, the name Walford apparently derived from the old word for "uncertain" or "wobbly", indicating that those using the ford were by no means certain of a dry crossing. It was a working mill until 1966, part of the vast Bankes Estate which includes the beautiful house of Kingston Lacy, and Corfe Castle in Purbeck. This was all bequeathed to the National Trust in 1982.

One year later, East Dorset District Council were able to buy the mill building and surrounding land. Renovations complete, Dorset Craft Guild took over the complex which is so ideally suited to its purpose.

The centre is now run as an independent education trust with a wide-ranging programme of courses and events. Details can be obtained from 01202-841400. There is a small but pleasant restaurant and a picnic area beside the River Stour.

Walford Mill Craft Centre, Wimborne.

STAPEHILL ABBEY (2)

A closed and silent order of nuns once lived and worked within these walls, between Wimborne and Ferndown. Now, the early 19th century Cistercian abbey has become a centre for craftsmen, surrounded by beautiful gardens. There are regular demonstrations of rural crafts and, if the children are bored, a home farm, woodland walk and adventure playground.

There is an admission charge; details from 01202-861686. The Abbey is open most of the year, although from October to Easter the times are more restricted.

COURTYARD CENTRE (3)

Emphasis is again placed on rural crafts at Lytchett Minster, four miles west of Poole Town Centre. Many crafts and hobbies are on display, with demonstrations and a chance to "have a go".

Garden centre, art gallery and pets corner make this a very full visit, with something for everyone. Open all year, except Christmas week.

WEYMOUTH CRAFT CENTRE (4)

Nearly three dozen crafts are on sale in a mini-market at Brewers Quay, Hope Square, not far from the harbour. You will also find traditional wooden items, from rocking horses to book ends, or be invited to throw your own pot out in the courtyard.

On the first floor, The Loft has a huge selection of everything from crafts to antiques, collectables and souvenirs.

Brewers Quay is open all year from 9.30 a.m. to 5.30 p.m.

DANSEL GALLERY, ABBOTSBURY (5)

Situated in one of Dorset's most picturesque villages, not far from the Swannery and Tropical Gardens, this craft gallery is filled with superb wooden items. Flowers, clocks, toys, mobiles - all are examples of the very best in design and quality of finish.

They'll make you want to touch and you'll certainly want to buy. There's absolutely no pressure to do so, though, and you're always made welcome to browse any day of the week. Winter opening times are slightly shorter, but 10 a.m. to 4 p.m. is a sure bet any season.

Dansel Gallery, Abbotsbury.

Broadwindsor craft centre.

BROADWINDSOR CRAFT AND DESIGN CENTRE (6)

In 1986 a group of redundant farm buildings began a new lease of life as a craft centre at Broadwindsor, close to Beaminster in the west of the county. The centre has grown, with an attractive restaurant and conservatory serving meals including Dorset Cream Teas.

The main shop sells a wide variety of crafts, while the adjacent workshops and studios are more specialised. Terry Whitworth's idiosyncratic watercolours, Lenschen's delicious hats, weather vanes, music - what a selection!

Open generally from 1 March to 23 December, but individual studios may vary.

The Pottery Tour

POOLE POTTERY (7)

Where it all began, but now with a reputation worldwide. Poole Pottery is on the Quay of what is now believed to be the world's largest harbour. There is a museum, factory tour, film, showrooms, well-stocked shop and a restaurant where you can relax after you've done it all.

The pottery is open throughout the year. If you want to take a tour and time is critical, give them a ring on 01202-666200 to check as tour times can vary according to season.

BLUE POOL (8)

Originally a clay pit which fed the potteries, the Blue Pool has become a popular beauty spot as well as being a Site of Special Scientific Interest. The tiny particles of clay in the pool, settling and rising again depending on the weather, cause brilliant light effects in the water through deep green to bright blue.

The museum tells the story of the clay industry in and around this particular estate, from clay pipes to fine ceramics. There are walks through twenty-five acres of fine countryside, so this is a lovely place to while away a couple of hours.

Open March to November from 9.30 a.m. Details of charges from 01929-551408.

ABBEY POTTERY, CERNE ABBAS (9)

In 1986 Paul Green moved to Dorset and began his pottery under the eye of the Cerne Giant. The emphasis is on a functional range of tableware which is oven and dishwasher proof and can also be used in a microwave.

Colours and textures vary but tend to be earthy with shape being all-important, enhanced perhaps by just a little subtle decoration. I particularly like the black/brown finish on some pieces, a combination of sophisticated gloss and rural form.

Abbey Pottery is usually open Tuesdays to Saturdays, from 10 a.m. to 6 p.m. Check if you are travelling a long distance on 01300-341865.

SHEPHERD'S WELL POTTERY, MOSTERTON (10)

The showroom at Mosterton, north-west of Beaminster, is full of delicious pieces by the Eeles family of potters. Wood-fired stoneware and porcelain, from large, useful vessels to tiny and delicate articles.

The showroom is open most days from 9 a.m. to 6 p.m. Ring on 01308-868257 for further information.

NEW BARN FIELD CENTRE (11)

The pottery of Poole comes full circle because here at Bradford Peverell the resident potter is Russel Sydenham. Together with his well-known father, potter Guy Sydenham, he learnt and perfected his skills at their island home in Poole Harbour.

Sea salt glaze and wood firing results in practical stoneware. Many items are on sale and you can also have a go at throwing your own pot.

The Field Centre, which also includes an Iron Age Homestead and Bygone Ways exhibition, is open from 10 a.m. every day, Easter to end of September. Further details from 01305-267463.

The Antiques Tour

BRIDPORT ANTIQUES CENTRE (12)

I love spending a morning in Bridport and wandering round its variety of shops. Parking is easy at the western end of town, which puts you close to Hobby Horse Antiques and the Bridport Antiques Centre in West Allington, Allington Fair Antiques in North Allington.

There are further antique shops in East Street and South Street.

DE DANAAN CENTRE, DORCHESTER (13)

A wide selection of antiques under one roof, from large items of furniture and beds to garden statues and Persian carpets. Smaller collectors' items, too, are tucked away in glass cabinets that ask to be explored. Don't be afraid to make an offer!

The centre is in London Road at the eastern edge of town. Open every day except Sunday.

OLD BUTTON SHOP ANTIQUES, LYTCHETT MINSTER (14)

Right off the beaten track, four miles from Poole Town centre, Mrs Thelma Johns runs this delightful little shop. The village saw a brief revival of the once thriving Dorset Button industry and this picturesque building has quite a history.

Not only does Mrs Johns display modern Dorset Buttons to show how they were made, but some of the rare, antique patterns are also on sale. Other old and decorative buttons plus a wonderful collection of small antiques make this a must for the enthusiast.

The shop is open week-days and Saturday mornings.

WIMBORNE ANTIQUES BAZAAR (15)

Three days a week, Wimborne draws the crowds to its market and antiques bazaar.

Fridays and Saturdays until lunchtime, Sundays 10 a.m. to 4 p.m., this is one of the largest markets in the south of England.

There is masses of free parking but the market is also well served by public transport. If you're looking for a bargain - don't miss it!

THE ANTIQUES NOOK, SHERBORNE (16)

Lots of interesting shops here, too, but you have to search them out. Try The Antiques Nook in South Street together with Heygate Browne Antiques. D&J Collectables are in Coldharbour, while Greystoke Antiques are in Cheap Street. On The Green is Richard White Antiques while Victor & Co are in Trendle Street.

The shops mentioned have a wide variety of stock and prices. You will find them all extremely helpful - but then shopping in Sherborne is always a pleasurable experience.

MARITIME INHERITANCE

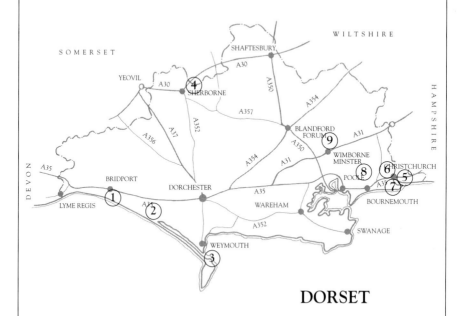

DORSET

THE NAVY TOUR
1. Rope and Net Museum, West Bay
2. Hardy's Monument, Blackdown
3. Portland Castle
4. Sherborne Castle

THE SMUGGLERS TOUR
5. Mudeford Quay
6. Mrs Perkins' mausoleum, Christchurch
7. Hengistbury Head
8. St. Andrew's Church, Kinson
9. Gulliver's tomb, Wimborne Minster

MARITIME INHERITANCE

Dorset's coast has always been connected with seafaring, both legal and illegal. As early as the 13th century the fleet's demand for ever-increasing supplies of ropes boosted Bridport's prosperity, based on the hemp and flax that were grown in the area. Their fibres were milled locally and then twisted in the rope-walks which gave the town its character. Although the industry stagnated on occasions, diversification into netting and sail-making kept the population busy.

There has been a port at West Bay since the 13th century, but it was never the deep water success of Weymouth and Poole. A constant battle was waged against silting up, which eventually led to its decline. The harbour was built in the 1770s.

As the Naval fleet grew, King Henry VIII recognised the importance of the waters around the Isle of Portland. It was at his instigation that Sandsfoot Castle and Portland Castle were built, between them covering the wide bay with a formidable protective firepower. Sandsfoot is now a picturesque ruin, but the solid Portland stone walls of the fort across the bay enclose a fascinating example of early coastal defence.

Queen Elizabeth I had her favourites, most notable among them being the sea captains that defended her shores and brought treasure from afar. Sir Walter Raleigh made his home in Dorset, at Sherborne Castle.

Friend and shipmate of Horatio, Lord Nelson, Admiral Sir Thomas Masterman Hardy was another of Dorset's notable seamen, while off the coast at the dead of night came those who have mostly gone unnamed but whose nocturnal activities brought many a keg of brandy, many a length of fine Brussels lace, ashore under the noses of the watching Excisemen.

The Navy Tour

WEST BAY, BRIDPORT: ROPE AND NETS (1)

West Bay is a small, enclosed harbour, full of the usual mix of small vessels that are to be seen in any seaside resort. Take a look at old photographs, though, and you will be surprised at the tall, masted schooners that used to ply their trade from here.

Adjacent is the Harbour Museum, very small but packed full of the early history of West Bay and neighbouring Bridport. You will see how the ropes and nets were made, and how Bridport developed around the long rope walks which can still be found today if you explore the back streets of the town. The museum is open from April to October and there is a small admission charge. (Further details 01308-420997.)

HARDY'S MONUMENT (2)

As Lord Nelson lay dying on the deck of HMS Victory at the Battle of Trafalgar, he uttered the famous phrase: "Kiss me, Hardy". While some still argue for other interpretations, there is no doubt whatsoever that the man to whom Nelson spoke is commemorated high on a Dorset hill.

West Bay.

Hardy's Monument on Blackdown, overlooking Chesil Beach, is a solid, Portland stone tower built to face and withstand the south-westerly winds. It is owned by the National Trust and the interior is open to the public. Views from the top on a clear day are remarkable, with the Devon coast visible to the west and the top of Bulbarrow to the north-east. The area around the Monument has lovely walks linking with the Coast Path.

Admiral Sir Thomas Masterman Hardy was born at nearby Kingston Russell house in 1769. He moved as a boy to the village of Portesham, at the bottom of Blackdown, until he joined the Royal Navy. Portesham House, his home, faces the main Weymouth/Bridport road. It is privately owned, although from time to time the gardens are open to the public.

Hardy's Monument on Blackdown.

PORTLAND CASTLE (3)

Part of a defence chain built from the Bristol Channel round the south coast and north to the Humber, Portland Castle was built about 1540 in the reign of Henry VIII. Following his Reformation, King Henry feared that European armies would be sent to re-establish Catholicism in England. His chain of defensive forts had mighty fire-power, Portland Castle mounting eighteen guns at several levels, and a captain of the Castle could expect to receive "16d a day for life".

Inscribed on the wall are the words: "God save King Henri the VIII of that name and Prinse Edward, begotten of Quene Jane: my Ladi Mari that goodly virgin and the Ladi Elizabeth so towardli, with the Kinges honorable counselors."

Together with the now ruined Sandsfoot Castle on the Weymouth shore, the fort guaranteed safe shelter within the bay. The precautions proved unnecessary, as the expected invasion never materialised. Charles II restored the building in 1703, placing his own coat of arms over the Tudor gateway.

The Castle is open from the end of March to October and there is an admission charge. (Further details 01305-820539.)

SHERBORNE CASTLE (4)

There are two castles at Sherborne, both associated with the famous seafarer and favourite of Queen Elizabeth I, Sir Walter Raleigh. The Old Castle dates from the 12th century and was the palace of Roger, Bishop of Salisbury. Raleigh bought the

Sherborne Castle.

estate in 1592 and decided conversion work was needed before he could settle here with his wife and son.

It proved too onerous a task, however, so Raleigh started work on the New Castle, the construction of which took about eight years as the main building took shape, then the corner turrets were added a few years later.

Sherborne proved a useful bolt-hole for Raleigh, whose marriage was kept secret from the Queen for as long as possible. When she discovered his 'unfaithfulness', a short spell in the Tower proved her displeasure. The Raleighs lived in Dorset until, once again, Sir Walter fell foul of the monarch. This time it was James I who sent him to the Tower, his Sherborne home forfeit, and his imprisonment led quickly to execution.

The New Castle is set in the rolling landscape planned by 'Capability' Brown. Leave plenty of time for a visit, from Easter Saturday through to the end of September, afternoons only, on Thursdays, Saturdays, Sundays and Bank Holiday Mondays. There is an admission charge. (Further details 01935-813182.)

The Smugglers Tour

MUDEFORD QUAY (5)

Picturesque at any time of year, the Quay flanks the narrow entrance into Christchurch Harbour with Hengistbury Head just a stone's throw away across the harbour mouth. The small group of cottages and the "Haven Inn" date back to the

Smuggler's refuge.

Mrs Perkins' mausoleum, Christchurch.

late 18th century when smuggling was in full swing.

One summer's night two smuggling luggers slipped in past the sandbar that made the entrance to the harbour such a tricky one to navigate. They unloaded brandy and tea which a willing army of helpers carried to a convoy of waiting wagons.

The sloop-of-war HMS Orestes was close at hand and her Captain sent six ship's boats with armed crew to apprehend the smugglers. Mr William Allen who was in command was mortally wounded as he stepped ashore, signalling the start of the Battle of Mudeford which reputedly lasted for fifteen hours with the smugglers holed up in the Haven Inn.

Remember that from Christchurch to Poole and for six miles inland was Bourne Heath. The chines that are now such a feature of Bournemouth stretched deep into the wild coastal cliffs. It is hardly suprising that the majority of smugglers went unmolested in their bid for a profit and were often helped by members of the public who stood to benefit from the "trade".

MRS PERKINS' MAUSOLEUM, CHRISTCHURCH (6)

While Christchurch was a well-documented landing place for smuggled goods, there is no hint that the Priory Church itself was ever used as a store for contraband. It was in a sad state of repair in the 17th and 18th centuries, with rustling colonies of bats which gave rise to fears that the area was haunted.

There was, however, the strange case of Mrs Perkins' mausoleum, the remains of which are now sited close to the Priory. Mrs Perkins died in 1783 after having often expressed a fear of being buried alive. She asked that instead of being interred her body be placed in a special building close to the Free School, which was then held in St. Michael's Loft in the Priory Church. This was so that the boys would hear her if she revived!

Mrs Perkins also asked that the lid of her coffin be left hinged and not screwed down, while the lock on the mausoleum door was to be made in such a way that she could open it herself from inside if necessary.

Her wishes were carried out and her mausoleum erected in the garden of a house called Church Hatch, close to the entrance to the Priory. Lieutenant-General Perkins died in 1803, at which time his wife's body was removed with his to the conventional family vault. The small but elaborately faced mausoleum was sold and re-erected in its present position, where its ruins are now used only by squirrels to hoard their winter feed.

Fear of ghosts and resurrections may indeed have kept people at a distance, but did this apply to the smuggling fraternity as well? Was this mausoleum a store for contraband, cloaked in respectability?

HENGISTBURY HEAD (7)

Archaeological evidence dates this as one of the earliest settled sites in the county and a trading port as early as 100 BC. The high sandy heathland separating the sea from Christchurch Harbour is now an important nature reserve. It was an important landfall for smugglers, who then worked their way inland across Bourne Heath with their casks and bundles.

In the late 18th century a Mr Warner of Christchurch recorded that he had seen on more than one occasion: "a procession of twenty or thirty waggons loaded with kegs of spirit ... winding deliberately and with most picturesque and imposing effect along the skirts of Hengistbury Head ... "

ST. ANDREW'S CHURCH, KINSON (8)

Kinson is now on the northern edge of Bournemouth, with the old church close to the River Stour. When just a small village surrounded by heathland it was well known to be on the route of smugglers heading inland with their goods.

St. Andrew's, Kinson, one of Gulliver's hiding places for contraband.

One of the best documented and notorious of these was Isaac Gulliver, who lived in Kinson for many years. His house, West Howe Lodge, was reputedly sited over a maze of tunnels and included a secret room that could only be accessed through a door halfway up a wide chimney flue. It was sadly demolished in the 1950s.

The squat tower of St. Andrew's Church was used for storing smuggled goods, the parapets being scored where ropes cut into the soft sandstone as kegs were hauled up and lowered down. The large chest tomb beside the church door also hid Gulliver's secrets behind its pivoted side. A tombstone on the opposite side of the church has a plaintive little verse in memory of Robert Trotman, "barbarously Murder'd" by the Revenue in 1765:

"A little Tea one leaf l did not steal.
For Guiltless Blood shed, I to God appeal.
Put Tea in one scale, human Blood in t'other
And think what tis to slay thy harmless Brother."

The verse emphasises the attitude of the day, that there was nothing wrong in a little smuggling to oil the wheels of commerce.

Although there were clashes which resulted in death and injury to smugglers and Revenue men alike, Gulliver's proud boast was that he and his men had never occasioned physical harm to anyone during his smuggling years. He commanded a large gang who openly displayed their 'uniform' of shepherd smock and long, powdered hair, earning them the name of White Wigs.

GULLIVER'S TOMB, WIMBORNE MINSTER (9)

Isaac Gulliver survived his smuggling days to become a respectable Dorset citizen. He remained in the wine trade and eventually married one of his daughters to a Wimborne banker. He became a churchwarden of the Minster and, when he died in 1822, was buried there. His memorial stone can be found in the north wall of the West Tower.

A TASTE OF DORSET

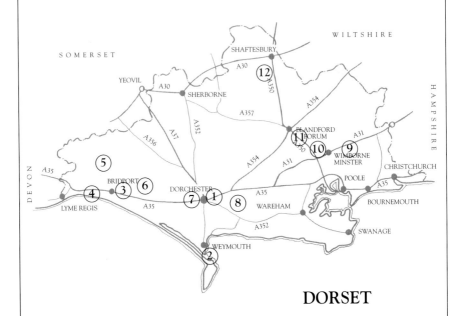

DORSET

THE SAVOURY TOUR
1. Eldridge Pope Brewery
2. Abbotsbury Oysters
3. Bridfish Smokery
4. Moores Dorset Knobs
5. Denhay cheddar and ham
6. Marquis of Lorne, Nettlecombe

THE SWEET TOUR
7. Dorchester Chocolates
8. Mill House Cider
9. Trehane Blueberries
10. Pamphill Farm Shop
11. Keynston Mill
12. The Cricketers, Shroton

A TASTE OF DORSET

Dorset boasts the very finest of delicacies to make your mouth water. Dairy products and hams are born of lush farmland, while fresh fish is the generous bounty of the sea.

Centuries of tradition lie behind the breweries, while elegant wines and gutsy cider add to the thirst-quenching choice.

You can crunch on savoury biscuits, fatten your waistline with chocolates, make blueberry pie and asparagus soup, all from the home produce that makes Dorset's table one of the best.

The following are just a few of the outlets that will be pleased to add enjoyment to your stay, or provide a treat to take home at the end of your holiday.

The Savoury Tour

ELDRIDGE POPE BREWERY, DORCHESTER (1)

The brewery on Weymouth Avenue fills the air with the smell of hops from time to time, as brews such as Thomas Hardy Ale are bottled for consumption near and far. The Green Dragon Brewery began in Acland Road 150 years ago with a strong-minded lady called Sarah Eldridge in charge of the great vats. The Pope family took over in 1861 and moved the business to Weymouth Avenue in 1879, where new premises were built in 1922.

"Full in body yet brisk as a volcano" was a description of Dorchester beer given by Thomas Hardy in one of his Wessex novels. As well as its traditional beers, Eldridge Pope also has a reputation for excellent wines which can be bought in the shop next to the brewery. Staff are always knowledgeable and are as happy to sell you a good bargain bottle as something rather more special.

A guided tour round the brewery is fascinating, but pre-booking is advisable especially during the peak holiday season. Ring 01305-251251 for further information.

If you are holidaying further west, Palmer's Brewery in Bridport also has tours of their premises. Ring 01308-427500 for days and times, which vary according to season.

ABBOTSBURY OYSTERS (2)

If you don't watch your spat, the starfish will eat them. No, it's not something from Trivial Pursuit, but one of the problems faced by Abbotsbury Oysters at their farm on Ferrybridge, between Weymouth and Portland.

The Fleet, the lagoon between the pebbly bank of Chesil Beach and the mainland, is a nature reserve and has been so since the days of King Canute. The pure waters play a major part in the growth of one million oysters a year, many of which are shipped throughout the UK on a 24 hour delivery service.

The Victorians loved them and Steak & Oyster Pie was a popular dish. Today oysters have a rather more expensive reputation, but at Abbotsbury Oysters they believe in keeping the prices as low as possible to encourage newcomers to try the delicacy at least once.

The baby oysters, or spat, begin life in a protected hatchery and are only transferred outside when they are sufficiently hardy. It takes two years to produce a fully fledged (probably not quite the right word) oyster, well fed on plankton. During the growing period the oysters are kept in mesh bags to deter starfish and crabs that have already developed a taste for them.

The final journey before they slip delightfully - raw or cooked - down someone's throat is through the purification tanks which make absolutely sure their quality remains of the highest order. If you would like to buy some or try some, a visit to Ferrybridge is a must. Instructions for opening and recipes which include oysters are always available. To take home or send to a gourmet friend, a wooden oyster barrel is an unusual choice. Further information can be obtained from Abbotsbury Oysters 01305-788867.

BRIDFISH SMOKERY (3)

At the roundabout to the east of Bridport centre, take the A3066 north towards Beaminster. Bridfish Smokery is on the left hand side, just a few hundred yards from the roundabout, on the Old Laundry Industrial Estate. If the wind is in the right direction, just sniff! Wonderful oak-smoking aromas will lead you there.

If it's possible to smoke it, Bridfish do so. Eels, chicken, kippers, pheasant, cod's roe, cheese, trout, duck ... The choice is as bewildering as it is delicious. Once you've tried something and are hooked, Bridfish can send to you by mail order with the minimum of fuss for next day delivery.

The mixed boxes are a special delight, making wonderful presents for friends (and for you, too). How about a Dorset Dream? It includes Denhay Cheddar, smoked salmon, Cerne Giant shortbread and apricot/stem ginger chutney. Or, for a scrummy picnic, smoked rainbow trout and prawns, duck breast and Cheddar wafers might fit the bill.

Bridfish can be contacted on 01308-456306. They are open 9-5 p m. Monday to Friday, 9-4 p.m. on Saturday.

MOORES DORSET KNOB BISCUITS (4)

There are several tasty biscuits in the Moores range, but they are famous for the crunchy Dorset Knobs in their distinctive tins. These were a traditonal start to the day for local farm workers when, in the mid-19th century, they were first baked by Eleanor and Samuel Moores at their small bakery in the Marshwood Vale.

Five of the couple's eleven children became bakers, one taking the secrets of Dorset Knobs as far away as St. Louis, Missouri. Samuel Junior founded the Morcombelake bakery on the present site in 1880 where the production of Dorset Knobs gradually overtook that of cake and bread.

Only made between January and March each year, each Knob is moulded by hand and undergoes three separate bakings to reach its crisp conclusion. They are sold in bags as well as tins and are an inexpensive and different holiday treat. Try them with a wedge of Blue Vinney cheese.

The bakery produces more than sixty thousand biscuits a day including the Gingers and Walnut Crunch biscuits that were a later addition to the range. These are fat and delicious and, once the packet is open, I bet you go on eating until you get to the bottom.

The bakery is open week-days throughout the year. It is on the south side of the A35, four miles west of Bridport.

DENHAY CHEDDAR AND HAM (5)

There is no Cheddar tastier than Denhay, from the Marshwood Vale in the west of the county. Denhay are proud that their experience over more than thirty years is recognised at such as the Royal Bath & West Show, where Challenge Trophies for farmhouse cheddar and a Champion Cheese award have been received.

Real Cheddar freaks can buy a 56lb traditional rinded cylinder, but more modest eaters may find the 4.5lb Dorset Drum easier to face. Denhay's advice is to keep it stored in a cool larder, allowing the cheese to reach room temperature before bringing it to table.

As a superb accompaniment, try Denhay's ham. Cured in, among other things, Dorset apple juice and honey, the hams are lightly smoked before being air-dried and sliced ready for sale.

Denhay Farm is at Broadoak, north-west of Bridport. There is a shop open on Mondays and Thursdays which also stocks other products fom the Dorset Harvest range. This group of producers guarantee to market the finest foods with "a natural, traditional taste"; a once tried, never forgotten range of preserves, biscuits, ice-cream and apple juice. They will be pleased to send you a Dorset Drum or some vacuum-packed ham by mail order if you've run out of holiday time. Ring 01308-422717.

MARQUIS OF LORNE, NETTLECOMBE (6)

After all that driving around buying up Dorset produce, let someone serve you a delicious meal so that you can sample the best the county has to offer before going home. There are pubs a-plenty; all good, many excellent.

The Marquis of Lorne - once you've found it - has a deserved reputation. Featured in the Good Pub Guide, Egon Ronay Guide to Pubs and Inns, the WHICH Guide to Country Pubs and the CAMRA Good Beer Guide, its selection of food, wines and beers is extensive.

From the A306 Bridport/Beaminster road, turn east just over a mile north of Bridport. Pass Mangerton Mill, through West Milton, straight on to Nettlecombe. Those of an adventurous nature driving from Dorchester should take the Roman road above Winterbourne Abbas to Eggardon hillfort, bear north and then south as you round the hillfort, following the signs for Powerstock. Straight through Powerstock and turn left for Nettlecombe.

The Sweet Tour

DORCHESTER CHOCOLATES (7)

Chocoholics are superbly catered for by The House of Dorchester. Recently moved to new premises at Poundbury, Prince Charles's "new village" on the Bridport Road, the company manufacture and box a mouth-watering selection for local consumption and also send them countrywide.

You can buy them at Stuart Turner, Tobacconist, in Tudor Arcade, off South Street, Dorchester.

MILL HOUSE CIDER (8)

Turn of the A352 between Dorchester and Wareham at Owermoigne, signposted to Crossways. Keep going until, on your left, you will see the sign for Mill House Nurseries. This is the place to come in the spring to stock up the garden, especially with an extensive range of fuchsias, but two interesting museums have also been developed on the site. One is the Dorset Collection of Clocks; the other is the Cider Museum.

This is a working museum with restored antique mills and presses which are used annually to produce both sweet and dry cider. There is a video explanation of the cider making process all year round.

The shop sells cider, of course, and also Somerset Royal Cider Brandy for something with a little more punch. Cheese, biscuits, ham, cider... You can make a real feast in Dorset.

The museum is open every day except the Christmas to New Year break, but double check on 01305-852220. There is a small admission charge to both museums, but parking is free. The shop is available to all.

TREHANE BLUEBERRIES (9)

Puddings, pies, wines; freeze them or prepare them fresh; blueberries are an unusual fruit which is rapidly gaining in popularity. At Trehane's, Hampreston Road, Ferndown, they are grown commercially for Marks & Spencer.

Visitors can buy ready-picked from the source, or Pick Your Own if you've time to spare. The season is from late July to late September.

PAMPHILL FARM SHOP (10)

On the outskirts of Wimborne, the hamlet of Pamphill is secluded and quiet. The ancient village green still attracts spectators for a Sunday afternoon game of cricket in the summer. The walking in and around the Kingston Lacy Estate is undemanding and scenic.

An old dairy and milking parlour have been converted into a range of excellent farm shops, with local produce as fresh as you could wish. Preserves, chutneys and Dorset cheeses; poultry, game and delicious sausages, local wine and Somerset cider; even a pets' pantry.

While the children play safely, adults can enjoy a cup of tea or coffee in the Parlour. Lunches and teas enable you to sample the shop produce before you decide which to take home.

Leave Wimborne on the B3082 to Blandford. The turning to Pamphill is on the left, very narrow, and the farm shop is a short distance from the main road on the right hand side. When you leave the shop, continue in the same direction and take the next turning left to the village green.

KEYNSTON MILL (11)

Wine from a Dorset vineyard and succulent asparagus draw regular customers back to Keynston Mill, halfway between Wimborne and Blandford off the B3082. At Tarrant Keynston, turn west at the crossroads signed Spetisbury. Follow the road past the church and on to the bank of the River Stour to find the Mill.

English Wine
Produced from grapes grown at
KEYNSTON MILL VINEYARD
BLANDFORD FORUM
DORSET

The Pick Your Own fields include fruit and vegetables. From 1st May to Mid-Summer's day especially, the asparagus season is in full swing. First class bundles for gourmet enjoyment; loose spears sold at about half the price; less than perfect spears, ideal for cooking into delicious soups.

The Partridge Vineyard produces a range of excellent white and sparkling wines. The shop and restaurant complete a day out, so take the opportunity to wander by the Stour and explore further afield. Opening times and information from 01258-452596.

THE CRICKETERS, SHROTON (12)

Off the A350 between Blandford and Shaftesbury, The Cricketers is another pub where you can be certain of a good meal and wide choice of wine and beer to drink. Shroton, or Iwerne Courtney, is situated on the River Iwerne that flows south to the Stour, close to Ham Hill.

Game and fish are the speciality, with a mouth-watering choice of puddings. If you want to be sure of an evening place, ring 01258-860421.

PICK AND MIX GEOGRAPHICAL INDEX

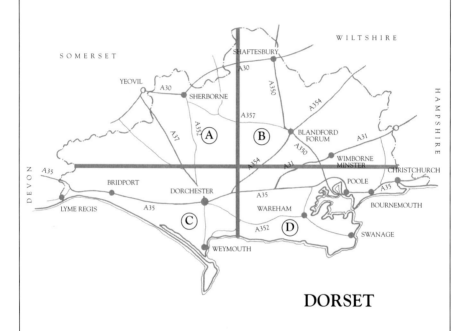

DORSET

PICK AND MIX GEOGRAPHICAL INDEX

C

D

TOURIST INFORMATION CENTRES

BLANDFORD
Marsh & Ham Car Park, West Street   Tel: 01258-454770

BOURNEMOUTH
Westover Road   Tel: 01202-451700

BRIDPORT
32 South Street   Tel: 01308-424901

CHRISTCHURCH
23 High Street   Tel: 01202-471780

DORCHESTER
Antelope Walk   Tel: 01305-267992

LYME REGIS
Guildhall Cottage, Church Street   Tel: 01297-442138

POOLE
The Quay   Tel: 01202-253253

SHAFTESBURY
8 Bell Street   Tel: 01747-853514

SHERBORNE
3 Tilton Court, Digby Road   Tel: 01935-815341

SWANAGE
The White House, Shore Road   Tel: 01929-422885

WAREHAM
Trinity Church, South Street   Tel: 01929-552740

WEYMOUTH
King's Statue, The Esplanade   Tel: 01305-785747

WIMBORNE
29 High Street   Tel: 01202-886116